Extreme Value Theory-Based Methods for Visual Recognition

Synthesis Lectures on Computer Vision

Editors
Gérard Medioni, *University of Southern California*
Sven Dickinson, *University of Toronto*

Synthesis Lectures on Computer Vision is edited by Gérard Medioni of the University of Southern California and Sven Dickinson of the University of Toronto. The series publishes 50- to 150-page publications on topics pertaining to computer vision and pattern recognition. The scope will largely follow the purview of premier computer science conferences, such as ICCV, CVPR, and ECCV. Potential topics include, but not are limited to:

- Applications and Case Studies for Computer Vision

- Color, Illumination, and Texture

- Computational Photography and Video

- Early and Biologically-inspired Vision

- Face and Gesture Analysis

- Illumination and Reflectance Modeling

- Image-Based Modeling

- Image and Video Retrieval

- Medical Image Analysis

- Motion and Tracking

- Object Detection, Recognition, and Categorization

- Segmentation and Grouping

- Sensors

- Shape-from-X

- Stereo and Structure from Motion

- Shape Representation and Matching

- Statistical Methods and Learning

- Performance Evaluation

- Video Analysis and Event Recognition

Extreme Value Theory-Based Methods for Visual Recognition
Walter J. Scheirer

ISBN: 978-3-031-00689-0   paperback
ISBN: 978-3-031-01817-6   ebook

DOI 10.1007/978-3-031-01817-6

A Publication in the Springer series
SYNTHESIS LECTURES ON COMPUTER VISION

Lecture #10
Series Editors: Gérard Medioni, *University of Southern California*
                              Sven Dickinson, *University of Toronto*
Series ISSN
Print 2153-1056   Electronic 2153-1064

Extreme Value Theory-Based Methods for Visual Recognition

Walter J. Scheirer
University of Notre Dame

SYNTHESIS LECTURES ON COMPUTER VISION #10

ABSTRACT

A common feature of many approaches to modeling sensory statistics is an emphasis on capturing the "average." From early representations in the brain, to highly abstracted class categories in machine learning for classification tasks, central-tendency models based on the Gaussian distribution are a seemingly natural and obvious choice for modeling sensory data. However, insights from neuroscience, psychology, and computer vision suggest an alternate strategy: preferentially focusing representational resources on the extremes of the distribution of sensory inputs. The notion of treating extrema near a decision boundary as features is not necessarily new, but a comprehensive statistical theory of recognition based on extrema is only now just emerging in the computer vision literature. This book begins by introducing the statistical Extreme Value Theory (EVT) for visual recognition. In contrast to central-tendency modeling, it is hypothesized that distributions near decision boundaries form a more powerful model for recognition tasks by focusing coding resources on data that are arguably the most diagnostic features. EVT has several important properties: strong statistical grounding, better modeling accuracy near decision boundaries than Gaussian modeling, the ability to model asymmetric decision boundaries, and accurate prediction of the probability of an event beyond our experience. The second part of the book uses the theory to describe a new class of machine learning algorithms for decision making that are a measurable advance beyond the state-of-the-art. This includes methods for post-recognition score analysis, information fusion, multi-attribute spaces, and calibration of supervised machine learning algorithms.

KEYWORDS

visual recognition, extreme value theory, machine learning, statistical methods, decision making, failure prediction, information fusion, score normalization, open set recognition, object recognition, information retrieval, biometrics, deep learning

Contents

Preface

The choice of a probability distribution can have a profound effect on the results coming from a model for an underlying analysis task—and not always in a good way. Consider the case of the 2008 financial crisis. Many different quantitative methods are deployed by economists and financial analysts to gauge the health of the economy. Some of these methods attempt to model the overall composition of a market sector, while others look at specific circumstances that may impact the market at large. A central tendency model would lead to an understanding of average market forces, and would have good predictive power when significant market forces move collectively in a certain direction (perhaps toward a bull or bear market).

An analyst using such a model back in 2007 would have had a rosy picture of the economy—a correction as large as the looming financial crisis was a seemingly improbable event. What eventually brought the financial system to the brink was a series of *extreme* market movements as firms holding mortgage-backed securities collapsed. An alternative modeling strategy would have focused not on average movement in the market, but on the tails of distributions representing specific market returns. Under such a model, where the extrema contribute to the model in a meaningful way, the financial crisis was well within the realm of possibility.

It is not an enormous leap of faith to believe that the same phenomenon occurs in computer vision. Most often we find that the extrema (e.g., edges, attributes, parts, salient objects) in a scene contained within a digital image define visual appearance, and not the average pixel content (*e.g.*, background). This calls for statistical modeling that does not deemphasize or ignore the rare facets of images or the features extracted from them. However in practice, this is not what we find. Remarkably, the field of computer vision has maintained a steady fixation with central tendency modeling, in spite of the complex nature of the underlying statistics of natural scenes. Extrema may be rare, but their influence is more often than not considerable.

These observations lead us to the topic at hand: the statistical extreme value theory. From predicting floods to downturns in the market, extreme value theory is a workhorse of predictive modeling in many fields outside of computer science. However, we are just starting to see its emergence within computer vision—an exciting and much welcomed development. Admittedly, there is some safety in central tendency modeling, as it allows one to invoke the central limit theorem, and assume that the normal distribution applies in approximation. But as we shall see, the first extreme value theorem functions in much the same way, and gives us access to a number of limiting distributions that apply in the tails of overall distributions, regardless of form. Given such flexibility, researchers within computer vision may find the extreme value theory becoming an indispensable part of their statistics toolkit once they get a feel for it.

This book is a summary of close to a decade of research into the application of the statistical extreme value theory to visual recognition. Unlike various references found in the statistics literature, it is intended to be a practical introductory guide to extreme value theory-based algorithms, and thus eschews proofs and other non-essential formalities. The interested reader is encouraged to dig deeper into the cited papers for that material as necessary. Further, this book can be read as a companion volume to the "Statistical Methods for Open Set Recognition" tutorial that was presented at CVPR 2016 in Las Vegas. The material from that tutorial, including slides and code, is available at the following URL: http://www.wjscheirer.com/misc/openset/. While this book represents a milestone of sorts for a budding research area within computer vision, we are sure to see even more intriguing work in this direction in the coming years.

Walter J. Scheirer
January 2017

Acknowledgments

I would like to extend my thanks to Gerard Medioni and Sven Dickinson, the editors of this Synthesis Lectures on Computer Vision series, for inviting me to contribute. I would also like to thank all of the researchers who granted me permission to use their figures in this book. Without their contribution, this volume would not have turned out as well as it did. I am also indebted to my editor, Diane Cerra, for her guidance and patience during the preparation of this manuscript. A group of expert reviewers from the field of machine learning provided helpful feedback that led to the polished version of the book that you have in your hands today. I am very grateful for their input. Finally, the idea for applying extreme value theory to recognition problems in computer vision came out of work undertaken at the University of Colorado, Colorado Springs and Securics, Inc. during the summer of 2008. The core group from that era of Terry Boult, Anderson Rocha, and Abhi Bendale remains instrumental to this research area—thanks for the great work and fun over the years, guys!

Walter J. Scheirer
January 2017

Figure Credits

Figure 1.2 (far left)	Based on: J. W. Tanaka and O. Corneille. Typicality effects in face and object perception: Further evidence for the attractor field model. *Perception & Psychophysics*, 69(4):619–627, May 2007.
Figure 1.2 (second from left)	Based on: D. Leopold, I. Bondar, and M. Giese. Norm-based face encoding by single neurons in the monkey inferotemporal cortex. *Nature*, 442:572–575, August 2006.
Figure 1.2 (middle)	Based on: J. W. Tanaka and M. J. Farah. Parts and wholes in face recognition. *Quarterly Journal of Experimental Psychology A: Human Experimental Psychology*, 46:225–245, 1993.
Figure 1.2 (second from right)	From: L. Itti and C. Koch. Computational modeling of visual attention. *Nature Reviews Neuroscience*, 2(3):194–203, February 2001. Copyright © 2001 Nature Publishing Group. Used with permission.
Figure 1.2 (far right)	From: E. Barenholtz and M. Tarr. Visual judgment of similarity across shape transformations: Evidence for a compositional model of articulated objects. *Acta Psychologica*, 128:331–338. Copyright © 2008 Elsevier. Used with permission.
Figure 3.1	From: W. J. Scheirer, A. Rocha, R. Michaels, and T. E. Boult. Meta-recognition: The theory and practice of recognition score analysis. *IEEE Transactions on Pattern Analysis and Machine Intelligence*, 33(8):1689–1695. Copyright © 2011 IEEE. Used with permission.
Figure 3.2	Based on: W. J. Scheirer, A. Rocha, R. Michaels, and T. E. Boult. Meta-recognition: The theory and practice of recognition score analysis. *IEEE Transactions on Pattern Analysis and Machine Intelligence*, 33(8):1689-1695, August 2011.
Figure 3.3	Based on: W. J. Scheirer, A. Rocha, R. Michaels, and T. E. Boult. Meta-recognition: The theory and practice of recognition score analysis. *IEEE Transactions on Pattern Analysis and Machine Intelligence*, 33(8):1689-1695, August 2011.

Figure 3.4   Based on: W. J. Scheirer, A. Rocha, R. Michaels, and T. E. Boult. Meta-recognition: The theory and practice of recognition score analysis. *IEEE Transactions on Pattern Analysis and Machine Intelligence*, 33(8):1689-1695, August 2011.

Figure 3.5a   Based on: W. J. Scheirer, A. Rocha, R. Michaels, and T. E. Boult. Meta-recognition: The theory and practice of recognition score analysis. *IEEE Transactions on Pattern Analysis and Machine Intelligence*, 33(8):1689-1695, August 2011.

Figure 3.6   Based on: V. Fragoso and M. Turk. SWIGS: A swift guided sampling method. In *IEEE Conference on Computer Vision and Pattern Recognition (CVPR)*, June 2013.

Figure 4.1   From: W. J. Scheirer, A. Rocha, R. Michaels, and T. E. Boult. Robust fusion: Extreme value theory for recognition score normalization. In *European Conference on Computer Vision (ECCV)*. Copyright © 2010 Springer-Verlag Berlin Heidelberg. Used with permission.

Figure 4.2   Based on: W. J. Scheirer, A. Rocha, R. Michaels, and T. E. Boult. Robust fusion: Extreme value theory for recognition score normalization. In *European Conference on Computer Vision (ECCV)*, September 2010.

Figure 4.3   From: V. Fragoso, P. Sen, S. Rodriguez, and M. Turk. EVSAC: Accelerating hypotheses generation by modeling matching scores with extreme value theory. In *IEEE International Conference on Computer Vision (ICCV)*. Copyright © 2013 IEEE. Used with permission.

Figure 4.4   From: X. Gibert, V. Patel, and R. Chellappa. Sequential score adaptation with extreme value theory for robust railway track inspection. In *Proceedings of the IEEE International Conference on Computer Vision Workshops*. Copyright © 2015 IEEE. Used with permission.

Figure 5.1   Based on: W. J. Scheirer, N. Kumar, P. N. Belhumeur, and T. E. Boult. Multi-attribute spaces: Calibration for attribute fusion and similarity search. In *IEEE Conference on Computer Vision and Pattern Recognition (CVPR)*, June 2012a.

Figure 5.2   From: W. J. Scheirer, A. Rocha, A. Sapkota, and T. E. Boult. Toward open set recognition. *IEEE Transactions on Pattern Analysis and Machine Intelligence*, 35(7):1757–1772. Copyright © 2013 IEEE. Used with permission.

Figure 5.3   From: L. P. Jain, W. J. Scheirer, and T. E. Boult. Multi-class open set recognition using probability of inclusion. In *European Conference on Computer Vision (ECCV)*. Copyright © 2014 Springer. Used with permission.

Figure 5.7   From: A. Bendale and T. E. Boult. Towards open set deep networks. In *IEEE Conference on Computer Vision and Pattern Recognition (CVPR)*. Copyright © 2016 IEEE. Used with permission.

CHAPTER 1

Extrema and Visual Recognition

The brain has the remarkable ability to rapidly and accurately extract meaning from a flood of complex and ever-changing sensory information. A key question is how neuronal systems encode relevant information about the external world, especially with respect to perceptual tasks such as object recognition and categorization. Unlocking this secret would likely change the typical way in which we approach machine learning for computer vision. In recent years, a powerful conceptual framework has emerged that posits that the brain fundamentally adapts itself to the statistics of the visual world, extracting relevant information from sensory inputs by modeling the distribution of inputs that are encountered. Investigations along this line have led to formal models including sparse coding (e.g., Olshausen and Field [1996, 2004], Vinje and Gallant [2000]) and deep learning (e.g., Bengio [2009], LeCun et al. [2015]), as well as a rekindled interest in perceptual models with explicit probabilistic interpretations (e.g., Berkes et al. [2011], Jern and Kemp [2013]). However, while such ideas may have revolutionized the way that we think about early sensory input, we have made little headway toward understanding the later stages of perceptual and cognitive processing that, for instance, enable a person to recognize or categorize objects and parse complex scene structure (see Cox [2014], DiCarlo and Cox [2007]). Such an understanding would enable more powerful artificial models for decision making in visual recognition.

In this book, a new model for visual recognition based on the statistical Extreme Value Theory (EVT) is introduced to satisfy some of the elements of later visual processing. In contrast to central-tendency modeling, it is hypothesized that distributions near decision boundaries form a more powerful model for recognition tasks by capturing the data that are arguably the most diagnostic features. EVT has several important properties: strong statistical grounding, better modeling accuracy near decision boundaries than Gaussian modeling (Fig. 1.1), the ability to model asymmetric decision boundaries, and accurate prediction of the probability of an event beyond our experience. After developing this theory, we will use it to describe a new class of machine learning algorithms for decision making that are a measurable advance beyond the state-of-the-art. These include methods for post-recognition score analysis, recognition score normalization, and the calibration of supervised machine learning algorithms. But first, let's take a look at the principal motivation behind EVT as a viable tool for visual recognition in computer vision.

1.1   AN ALTERNATIVE TO CENTRAL TENDENCY MODELING

From early representations in the brain, to highly abstracted class categories in machine learning, models based on the Gaussian distribution, central tendency, or expected values are a common and seemingly natural choice for modeling sensory data. However, insights from neuroscience (e.g., Freiwald et al. [2009], Groen et al. [2012], Leopold et al. [2006], Tsao and Livingstone [2008]), psychology (e.g., Leopold et al. [2001], Scholte et al. [2009], Tanaka et al. [2012]), and computer vision (e.g., Fragoso and Turk [2013], Fragoso et al. [2013], Scheirer et al. [2011, 2012a, 2014a]) suggest an alternate strategy: preferentially focusing representational resources on the extremes of the distribution, which include the data closest to any decision boundaries (Fig. 1.1).

Existing rational theories of category learning (e.g., Ashby and Alfonso-Reese [1995], Danks [2007], Griffiths et al. [2007, 2011], Rosseel [2002]) formulate the core problem of recognition as determining the probability distributions over stimuli associated with different category labels. Such models are dominated by the average data, despite the fact that behaviorally relevant information is often found far from the mean, toward the decision boundary between visual classes. While other distributions can and have been used, including more complicated mixture models, using any density model with central tendency estimation focuses on the less relevant "expected data." Furthermore, density estimation requires that the samples reasonably cover the space, yet myriad experiments have shown a cognitive ability to extrapolate far from the training data. Thus we eschew direct density estimation.

In contrast to central tendency modeling (e.g., Gaussian modeling), here it is proposed that models based on the statistical EVT (Kotz and Nadarajah [2001]) can form a powerful basis for recognition or categorization, focusing on the deviations from the average that are arguably the most diagnostic features for performing recognition, while simultaneously enforcing sparsity in the models. The EVT, combined with data from extrema around decision boundaries, can provide the distributional approximations needed for visual perception, recognition and category learning.

The key to EVT modeling is that the extreme value theorem limits what functional forms must be considered. Much as the central limit theorem provides support for Gaussians in some problems, EVT defines what parametric distribution the data near the decision boundary must follow. In this book, we will assume that those data are 1D random variables (e.g., decision scores). This allows effective fitting with partial data—we do not need to see most of the data, just the extrema. Of course, it is often difficult to observe extrema in practice, because they tend to be rare random variables. However, since the dawn of the so-called "big data era," our chance of observing extreme data is much higher for many problems, and thus EVT can be invoked more regularly. EVT has been used for decades in other fields, but recent work has identified it as a tool for recognition and learning. Scheirer et al. [2011] showed that most recognition problems are consistent with the EVT. While this proposed work has very broad implications, from full models of category learning to hierarchical/deep learning models, to addressing the role of sparsity, the scope of our discussion here will be limited to the development of a theory for visual recognition that will be used to develop a new class of tools for supervised machine learning.

In essence, a new unifying model is being proposed, wherein extreme values are used to build distributional prototypes. It is unifying because the EVT-based model addresses both the long-standing split between exemplar/prototype and discriminative/generative models, using the data near the boundaries (i.e., extrema) to build probabilistic models that can then be used for discrimination. Since EVT needs only a few extreme samples to model the probabilities, it partially sidesteps the question of abstraction—it has the compactness of an abstraction yet uses a few samples.

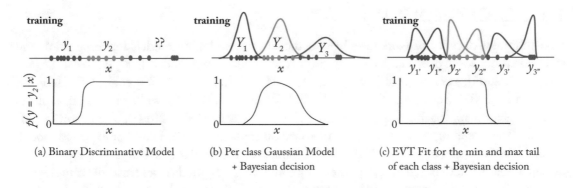

(a) Binary Discriminative Model

(b) Per class Gaussian Model + Bayesian decision

(c) EVT Fit for the min and max tail of each class + Bayesian decision

Figure 1.1: Overview of the fundamental idea of this book: an extreme value theory for visual recognition. The first column (a) shows data from two known classes, and a hypothetical discriminative model that could be learned from that data to separate class y_2 from y_1. However, a problem with this model is that positive classification continues beyond the reasonable support of y_2, including a third class (shown in blue). The second column (b) shows a Gaussian distribution fit as a generative model of that data and the resulting conditional decision function (generalized from Jern and Kemp [2013] to three classes). Note the green points from data x labeled Y_2 have a cluster near the data labeled Y_1 and other points farther away—because the region is wide, it yields weaker discrimination. The conditional decision function near Y_1 and Y_2 is impacted by data quite far from that decision boundary. The alternative proposed in this book, column (c), uses statistical EVT to estimate the probability distributions. With EVT, estimates are made separately for the tails at each decision boundary for a class, e.g., one for the lower decision boundary y'_i, and another for the upper decision boundary y''_i. With different shapes (EVT peaks with strongest discrimination near a class boundary, and the Gaussian peaks in the middle of the data), very testable hypotheses can be evaluated. Missing from prior work is the question of multi-class interaction and when/how the conditional estimates drop back to zero, as well as how much the upper decision boundary data impacts the shape of the lower decision boundary. Gaussians have full support, while EVT depends only on the tails, yielding additional testable hypotheses. The advantage of EVT fitting is that it provides better decision boundaries, i.e., greater discrimination, while requiring fewer statistical assumptions.

In Fig. 1.1, some key advantages of this approach are highlighted: support for multiple classes, better modeling accuracy near decision boundaries than traditional Gaussian generative modeling, the ability to model asymmetric decision boundaries (which are common in many visual categorization tasks), and the ability to accurately predict the probability of a rare event or new event beyond our current experience. A flexible model that adapts itself to the data around the decision boundaries is a primary contribution of this work. In Fig. 1.1, one can see that y_2', which has three closely spaced points near the decision boundary, has a sharp transition, but y_1'' has a slower transition because there is a greater spread at the boundary. Such abstract evidence is nice, but what more concrete clues do we have that the EVT applies to visual recognition problems?

1.2 BACKGROUND

In psychology, decades of work have been dedicated to developing models for recognition and categorization, some of which focuses on prototype or rule-based models (e.g., Ashby and Maddox [1993, 2005], Leopold et al. [2006], Minda and Smith [2011], Nosofsky et al. [1994a], Smith and Minda [2002], Squire and Knowlton [1995], Wallis et al. [2008]), while other work explores exemplar-based approaches (e.g., Kruschke [1992], Nosofsky [1991, 2011]). The prototype approaches for modeling sensory statistics are based on capturing the "average" or expected model, generally by Gaussian or multinomial modeling, and measure similarity to the various models. The exemplar-based models generate hypotheses by combining weighted values from all examples and measure similarity during recognition or categorization. Both have advantages and disadvantages and experiments have been performed that support each type. In general, exemplar-based models provide a better fit to the data, but the main concern raised against the exemplar approach is its lack of cognitive economy. A few proposed models have even been based on statistically *ad hoc* combinations of rule-based exemplars (e.g., Nosofsky et al. [1994b]), conversion of prototypes into pre-specified algebraic decision bounded models (e.g., the quadratics of Ashby and Maddox [1993]), or hybrid prototypes with exemplars (e.g., Griffiths et al. [2007], Love et al. [2004], Vanpaemel and Storms [2008]). These hybrid models use classical exponential, Gaussian, or Dirichlet distributions, estimated using central tendencies of clustered data. In summary, the long-standing debate on theories for category representation involves a tension between informativeness and economy (Vanpaemel and Storms [2008]). We can conjecture that this tension is driven by the poor ability of central tendency-based or low-order algebraic models/rules to capture the decision boundaries in a general sense. However, for simple stimuli or small sample sizes, the rule-based systems often better explain the data, leading to hybrid models that are purely empirical. By defining the prototype distributions using statistically grounded EVT, we expect to attain better informativeness while achieving better economy in a theoretical model that unifies multiple past models.

The notion of treating extrema near a decision boundary as features is not necessarily new, but a comprehensive statistical theory of recognition that uses the extrema as a foundation is. The field of vision science has witnessed a surge in work asking more detailed questions about the

Extrema as Features

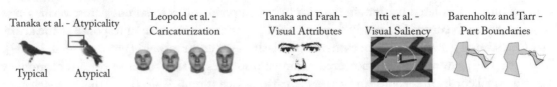

Figure 1.2: A broad body of prior work suggests that extrema draw our attention, providing useful information for visual recognition tasks. Most visual content is not information rich and is likely discarded as part of a strategy to enforce economy/sparsity. Recent work has examined the extrema from part boundaries (Barenholtz and Tarr [2008]), object atypicality (Tanaka and Corneille [2007], Tanaka et al. [1998, 2011, 2012]), and caricaturization (Freiwald et al. [2009], Leopold et al. [2006], Tanaka and Simon [1996]) that drive strong neuron population responses, as well as visual attributes (Going and Read [1974], Peterson and Rhodes [2003], Tanaka and Farah [1993], Valentine [1991]) and visual saliency (DeWinter and Wagemans [2008], Einhäuser et al. [2008], Itti and Koch [2001], Stirk and Underwood [2007]).

nature of the image representation and the response it elicits in the brain. To establish a basis, objects are often placed into a face- or shape-space (Leopold et al. [2005, 2006]) where a norm or average object is found in the center, and different feature trajectories branch out to emphasize certain geometric traits. Observing this space, we can ask if averages or extremes become models for visual recognition (e.g., Bartlett et al. [1984], Leopold et al. [2001], Rosch et al. [1976]). The work of Tanaka et al. (Bartlett and Tanaka [1998], Tanaka and Corneille [2007], Tanaka et al. [1998, 2011, 2012]) has explored this question in depth, casting what is extreme as "atypicality," which has been shown to draw more human attention than typical exemplars. In experiments with faces and objects (Tanaka et al. [2012]), when an average representation is created from typical and atypical images for the same object class, it is almost always considered by human subjects to be closer to the atypical image (likely based on correspondence between at least one extreme feature; see the example of the bird in Fig. 1.2). This effect led Tanaka et al. [1998] to pursue the model of an "attractor field" centered around the extremes in a sparse sub-region of object space. Controlling for the category learning bias by using artificial "blob" objects, Kantner and Tanaka [2012] were able to replicate the findings from the experiments that used natural objects, suggesting that the phenomenon of directed attention toward atypicality is fundamental to recognition.

Similarly, caricature effects are thought to play a very strong role in face recognition (Lee et al. [2000], Leopold et al. [2006], Lewis and Johnston [1998], Mauro and Kubovy [1992], Tanaka and Simon [1996]) because they over-emphasize certain traits that can be matched easily. This type of asymmetric, extrema-based tuning has been observed in higher visual cortex. Leopold et al. [2006] made two important observations in this context. First, at a psychophysical level, experiments show that as the degree of caricaturization increases, so does recognition accuracy. Second, to explore this psychophysical observation at a neural level, Leopold et al. measured the responses of isolated neurons in anterior inferotemporal cortex to stimuli across various axes of a face space. Neurons frequently demonstrated a monotonic increase in response as the artificial face stimuli grew to be more extreme. Similarly, Tsao and Freiwald (Freiwald et al. [2009], Tsao and Livingstone [2008]) measured neuronal responses in face selective regions of monkey ventral visual cortex in response to parametric cartoon face stimuli. They found that face-selective neurons frequently responded most vigorously to extreme faces, monotonically increasing firing up to the extremes of what could still be considered a face. Such results provide tantalizing clues that neuronal representations might be explicitly tuned toward representing extremes, including stimuli that are rarely (or even never), experienced.

A dichotomy in the literature which is directly addressed by the ideas this book will introduce is the apparent split between discriminative and generative models. The strengths and weaknesses of each have been extensively discussed by psychologists and vision researchers (e.g., Ashby and Alfonso-Reese [1995], Jern and Kemp [2013], Kruschke [2011], Pothos and Bailey [2009], Tu [2007], Ulusoy and Bishop [2005], Zhu [2003]). Traditionally, generative models are more difficult to build and often assume a parametric form, e.g., a Gaussian or a mixture model, which focuses on the most common data, and has difficulty fitting near the decision boundary. It should also be noted that there can be some confusion in terminology. In practice, the term discriminative is also used to describe training using data near the class boundaries (Colwill and Rescorla [1988], Estes [1943]) to produce a model well-suited to discrimination of classes.

Interestingly, within the vision science literature one finds multiple examples where Extreme Value Distributions (EVDs) are used to fit experimental results (e.g., Bao et al. [2010], Debbabi et al. [2012], Furmanski and Engel [2000], Groen et al. [2012], Hebart et al. [2012], McAlonan et al. [2008], Quick [1974], Reynolds et al. [2000], Scholte et al. [2009], Watson [1979]). For instance, the cumulative distribution function of the Weibull distribution is frequently used to fit psychometric and neurometric curves. While this usage is sometimes connected to probability summation (Quick [1974], Watson [1979]), the choice of the Weibull is often a matter of fitting expedience, rather than invoking any deep organizing theory. Likewise, EVDs have been suggested as computationally efficient means to explain scene content (Zografos and Lenz [2011]). Nonetheless, this use of EVDs, along with others, indicates a running undercurrent in the literature, where EVDs are used to model data in neuroscience and psychology.

1.3 EXTREME VALUE THEORY FOR RECOGNITION

Problems considering extreme values (i.e., those that deviate from the norm) are named extreme value problems. These problems consider the distribution of the extreme values from a population, e.g., maximum similarity or minimum distance. The first EVT is analogous to a central limit theorem, but tells us what the distribution of extreme values should look like as we approach the limit. Extreme value distributions are the limiting distributions that occur for the maximum (*or* minimum, depending on the data) of a large collection of random observations from an arbitrary distribution. A number of related problems exist, some of which are well addressed by EVT models. These include outlier detection (Rousseeuw and Leroy [2005]), anomaly detection (Chandola et al. [2009]), and risk management (Rasmussen [1997]).

Gumbel [1954] showed that for any continuous and invertible initial distribution, only three EVT models are needed, depending on whether the maximum or the minimum is of interest, and also if the observations are bounded from above or below. The three types of EVDs can be unified into a generalized extreme value (GEV) distribution given by

$$GEV(t) = \begin{cases} \frac{1}{\lambda} e^{-v^{-1/\kappa}} v^{-(1/\kappa+1)} & \kappa \neq 0 \\ \frac{1}{\lambda} e^{-(x+e^{-x})} & \kappa = 0, \end{cases} \tag{1.1}$$

where $x = \frac{t-\tau}{\lambda}$, $v = (1 + \kappa \frac{t-\tau}{\lambda})$, and κ, λ, and τ are the shape, scale, and location parameters, respectively. Different values of the shape parameter yield the extreme value type I, II, and III distributions. Specifically, the three cases $\kappa = 0$, $\kappa > 0$, and $\kappa < 0$ correspond to the Gumbel (I), Frechet (II), and Reversed Weibull (III) distributions. An understanding of how these distributions are bounded gives us some intuition into how they may be applied in practice (National Institute of Standards and Technology [2012]). Gumbel has infinite extent and is for distributions of infinite support, Frechet is zero for $t \leq \tau$ and is for maxima from distributions with support bounded from below but unbounded above (e.g., response time), and the Reversed Weibull is for maxima of data bounded from above (e.g., maximum similarity). The Weibull is often used to model data bounded from below (e.g., minimum distance). Note that all of these distributions are of infinite extent on one or both ends; data bounded from above and below can be modeled by combining extrema, maxima, and minima, with the result requiring a mixture of Reversed Weibull and Weibull distributions.

The most crucial aspect of EVT is that independent of the choice of model for the overall distribution, we don't have to assume a distributional model for any given distribution around a decision boundary because we know it must be in the EVT family. In other words, no matter what model best fits all of the data, be it a truncated binomial, a truncated mixture of Gaussians, a log-normalized value, a sum of correlated random variables (Bertin and Clusel [2006]), or even a complicated but bounded multi-modal distribution, with enough samples and enough classes the sampling of the data points closest to the decision boundary always results in an EVT distribution of a known functional form. The way to prove if EVT is applicable is the following: one has to show that the limiting distribution of extreme values of the underlying distribution exists. In the case where it exists, then the distribution always is the GEV. It is true that for the known parametric distributions this limit exists. Classical EVT assumes i.i.d. samples, but can be generalized to the weaker assumption of exchangeable random variables (Berman [1962]).

Using this observation, the rest of this book will make extensive use of two models, the Probability of Inclusion ($\iota = $ positive) and Probability of Exclusion ($\varepsilon = $ negative). These models can be combined into a $P_{\iota\varepsilon}$ model (Scheirer et al. [2014a]), which is the product seeking the probability that something is from the positive class and not from the negative class. Further, we can combine $P_{\iota\varepsilon}$ with prior class probabilities to get the overall (unnormalized) posterior P_π. To start, assume a hypothesis similarity $s_\iota(x, c)$ such that a sample x is included in class c, and a hypothesis score $s_\varepsilon(x, c)$ such that x should be excluded from c, where we assume larger scores imply more likely inclusion/exclusion.

While it is straightforward to develop the decision model for any EVT distribution, for simplicity of presentation let us assume the inclusion scores are bounded from below and the exclusion scores bounded above, which dictates the distribution for the extremes to be a Weibull and Reversed Weibull, respectively. Note in both cases we are using only a few extreme values to fit the long-tail of the distribution, not its bounded half.

To estimate the probability for any score x belonging to class c, we can use the appropriate cumulative distribution function with the associated parameters. Given x, we have two independent estimates: one for inclusion, P_ι, based on the Weibull Cumulative Distribution Function (CDF) derived from the match data for class c, and another for exclusion, P_ε, based on the Reversed Weibull CDF from the non-match estimates for class c. This yields a class conditional density estimation, the Probability Inclusion Exclusion estimate $P_{\iota\varepsilon}$, defined by the product

$$
\begin{aligned}
P_{\iota\varepsilon}(x|c, \theta_c) &= P_\iota(x|c, \theta_{\iota_c}) \times P_\varepsilon(x|c, \theta_{\varepsilon_c}) \\
&= (1 - e^{-(\frac{s_\iota(x,c) - \tau_{\iota_c}}{\lambda_{\iota_c}})^{\kappa_{\iota_c}}}) \cdot (e^{-(\frac{s_\varepsilon(x,c) - \tau_{\varepsilon_c}}{\lambda_{\varepsilon_c}})^{\kappa_{\varepsilon_c}}}),
\end{aligned}
\tag{1.2}
$$

where θ_c represents the parameters for both Weibull fits. For a given stimulus, the approach is thus to find the nearby extrema from the different classes, compute $P_{\iota\varepsilon}$, and then predict the class with the maximum probability. We may also choose to report "unknown" if all estimates are below some threshold.

It is worth noting that the difference between the fit of a non-EVT central-tendency oriented distribution and an EVT distribution is often very significant. An example of this is shown in Fig. 1.3, with data from a two-class discrimination task along a parametric stimulus axis. Similarly, EVT should easily be distinguished from a simple rule-based model, a General Recognition Model (Ashby and Maddox [1993], Ashby and Perrin [1988]) or exemplar-based General Context Model (GCM) (Nosofsky [2011]), using an experimental protocol like that of Rouder and Ratcliff [2004] and Nosofsky and Little [2010].

The motivation for this book comes from recent advances in machine learning (Fragoso and Turk [2013], Fragoso et al. [2013], Jain et al. [2014], Scheirer et al. [2011, 2012a, 2014a]), which showed that most recognition problems are consistent with the EVT. In particular, in Scheirer et al. [2012a], a model for any generalized decision boundary was introduced and applied to similarity computation using visual facial attributes. This is a concrete example of the applicability of EVT theory for visual recognition at the decision boundary for a real-world problem containing unconstrained imagery from the web. With a variety of asymmetric recognition effects (Tversky [1977], Tversky and Gati [1982], Tversky and Koehler [1994]) when matching across multiple dimensions, the attribute recognition problem is a particularly interesting and challenging case for EVT modeling. We'll look at this example in more detail in Chapter 5.

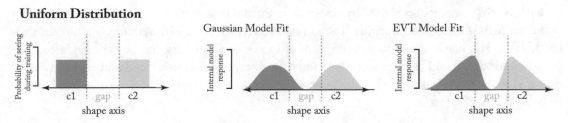

Figure 1.3: An example two-class discrimination task along a parametric stimulus axis. Left-hand panel: the probability of drawing examples from class 1 (c1) during training is shown in red, and the probability of drawing class 2 (c2) is shown in blue. In all conditions, a gap region where no training examples were shown is imposed between the two categories. The middle panel shows Gaussian model fit predictions for each training distribution, and the third panel shows corresponding EVT model fits. Importantly, there is a large difference between the fits of the Gaussian and EVT models.

In summary, the assumptions necessary to apply EVT to a visual recognition problem are that we have sufficiently many extrema providing support near the decision boundary for the approximation in the limit to apply. To use EVT, we need not know or assume the parametric form of the data, nor the parameters of the similarity distribution—we only assume it exists and is a proper distribution, and that we can identify the extrema.

1.4   DECISION MAKING IN MACHINE LEARNING

Since the release of the result by Krizhevsky et al. [2012] on the ImagetNet Large Scale Visual Recognition Challenge 2012 [ILSVRC2012], the visual recognition community has placed a nearly singular focus on representation learning. The prevailing sentiment is that the fundamental problem of recognition can be solved by combining representation learning and reasoning via operations on large vectors (LeCun et al. [2015]). However, there is strong evidence (Nguyen et al. [2015], Szegedy et al. [2014], Tsai and Cox [2015]) that weak decision boundary modeling is a persistent problem that leads to class confusion. It can be suggested that the current strategies for read-out layers in artificial neural networks are limiting factors. There is nothing inherent in neural network theory to support linear Support Vector Machine (SVM) or the Softmax function as a read-out layer for models of visual perception that must support open set recognition problems like detection, one-shot learning problems with extremely limited samplings of positive training data, and problems with hierarchical classes or class overlap. It is readily apparent that we do not understand decision boundary modeling as well as we should.

In this book, more attention is given to decision making at an algorithmic level to address the limitations of existing classification techniques. Unique to this discussion, we will leave open the possibility of a new theory of biological visual discrimination framed by the above discussion of evidence from the natural world. Neuroscience may hold the key to achieving the next breakthroughs in computer vision: by using the brain as a frame of reference, we have access to a powerful pattern recognition engine that solves visual recognition with seemingly effortless ability. If EVT is indeed an accurate description of the decision making used by the brain to learn class boundaries, it will become a unified model for discrimination in natural and artificial recognition systems as we design and evaluate new algorithms that exhibit the same characteristics as biological model systems.

1.5   ORGANIZATION

In the following chapters, a concise introduction to EVT for visual recognition and its application to machine learning-based decision making is presented. Chapter 2 provides a brief review of the statistical EVT, including the theory and distributions that apply to computer vision. Chapter 3 makes use of the theory to develop a methodology for post-recognition score analysis—a way to make an algorithmic matching decision without the need for traditional thresholds. Chapter 4 extends the idea of post-recognition score analysis to recognition score normalization for information fusion, whereby heterogeneous data can be combined in a consistent manner to improve automatic recognition. Chapter 5 in turn extends the mechanisms of score normalization to calibration for supervised machine learning algorithms, which facilitates open set recognition and more interpretable decision values. Chapter 6 summarizes the contributions of this volume and suggests future directions for EVT in computer vision. The EVT-based algorithms for visual recognition that will be discussed in the remainder of this book are summarized in Table 1.1.

Table 1.1: A summary of the EVT-based algorithms for visual recognition discussed in this book

EVT-based Method	Purpose
Meta-Recognition Scheirer et al. [2011], Chpt. 3	Weibull-based tail modeling for recognition system failure prediction.
Rayleigh Meta-Recognition Fragoso and Turk [2013], Chpt. 3	Rayleigh-based tail modeling for predicting failure in image correspondence problems.
W-score Normalization Scheirer et al. [2010], Chpt. 4.	Weibull-based tail modeling for recognition score normalization.
EVSAC Fragoso et al. [2013], Chpt. 4.	Extreme value sample consensus via GEV-based normalization.
GEV K-means Li et al. [2012], Chpt. 4.	Improved K-means clustering algorithm meant to better tolerate outliers.
Pareto-based Normalization for Outlier Detection Furon and Jégou [2013], Chpt. 4.	Outlier detection methodology that normalizes scores coming out of a CBIR system.
Pareto-based Normalization for Visual Inspection Gibert et al. [2015b], Chpt. 4.	Estimation of an adaptive threshold from GPD fit to score data.
Multi-Attribute Spaces Scheirer et al. [2012a], Chpt. 5.	Calibration for binary classiers applied to closed set recognition problems.
PI-SVM Jain et al. [2014], Chpt. 5.	Weibull-based Probability of Inclusion calibration for binary classifiers applied to open set recognition problems.
W-SVM Scheirer et al. [2014a], Chpt. 5.	Weibull-based Probability of Inclusion and Exclusion calibration for binary classifiers applied to open set recognition problems.
Sparse Representation-based Open Set Recognition Zhang and Patel [2017], Chpt. 5.	Pareto-based calibration of the matched reconstruction error distribution and the sum of non-matched reconstruction error.
OpenMax Bendale and Boult [2016], Chpt. 5	Weibull-calibrated decision function for convolutional neural networks.

CHAPTER 2

A Brief Introduction to Statistical Extreme Value Theory

An important question to ask before applying EVT to a particular problem is when does it apply in a formal sense? Fundamentally, the answer is when the distribution to be modeled consists of extrema. As emphasized above in Chapter 1, extrema are the minima or maxima sampled from an overall distribution of data. To quote Coles [2001] "The distinguishing feature of an extreme value analysis is the objective to quantify the stochastic behavior of a process at unusually large—or small—levels." Assume a sequence of i.i.d. samples $(s_1, s_2, \ldots)$. The maximum over an n-observation period is thus:

$$M_n = \max(s_1, s_2, \ldots). \tag{2.1}$$

For large values of n, the approximate behavior of M_n follows from the limit arguments associated with n approaching infinity. From this observation, an entire family of models can be calibrated via the observed extrema values of M_n.

In this chapter, we will walk through a simple example to emphasize the quantitative difference between central tendency modeling and EVT modeling. We will then go on to introduce the Extreme Value Theorem, and discuss the circumstances under which it applies. Building from the extreme value theorem, we will then look at the various distributions defined directly by the theorem, and other related distributions that have been applied to problems in computer vision. For a good fit, accurate tail size estimation is essential, thus we examine strategies for this. Finally, we take a look at some important considerations for the examination of visual data with respect to the assumptions necessary to apply EVT. This chapter is meant to be a brief introduction to this quite expansive field of statistics. Many good and accessible references on EVT are available. The interested reader is encouraged to seek out the following references: Coles [2001], de Haan and Ferreira [2007], Gumbel [1954], National Institute of Standards and Technology [2012].

2.1 BASIC CONCEPTS

To begin, let's look at a very basic step-by-step example showing the difference in probability estimation between tail modeling and central tendency modeling. In Chapter 1, we saw in a conceptual sense that the difference between fits can be drastic (Fig. 1.3). Here we look at the numerical difference. The R environment[1] is a convenient tool for statistical modeling, and it includes specific packages for extreme value theory modeling. The following examples are written in the R language, but should be understandable to any reader with a basic computer programming background.

The central limit theorem tells us that the arithmetic mean of a sufficiently large number of i.i.d. variables, each with a well-defined expected value and variance, will approximately follow a normal (i.e., Gaussian) distribution, regardless of the underlying distribution. This can be demonstrated by sampling from a specified distribution, and taking the mean of each sample set n number of times. The code below samples 1,000 values from a standard normal distribution, computes the mean for that set of samples, and stores it. This process is repeated 10,000 times.

```
nsamples <- 1000
ntrials <- 10000
bufferMean <- vector(length=ntrials)

for (i in 1:ntrials) {
  # sample from an overall normal distribution
  y <- rnorm(nsamples,mean=0,sd=1)
  # store the mean from each set of samples
  bufferMean[i] <- mean(y)
}
```

When we plot the histogram of the means stored in bufferMean, we see the familiar bell-shaped curve associated with central-tendency models (Fig. 2.1). Its peak is at 0, which matches the mean of the normal distribution we sampled from. This is exactly what we expect after sampling the means, because the central limit theorem holds in this case. But what happens if we compute and store the maximum of each set of samples, instead of the mean?

```
bufferMax <- vector(length=ntrials)

for (i in 1:ntrials) {
  # sample again from an overall normal distribution
  y <- rnorm(nsamples,mean=0,sd=1)
  # store the max from each set of samples
  bufferMax[i] <- max(y)
}
```

The resulting histogram in Fig. 2.2 looks much different than the histogram in Fig. 2.1—no longer do we see a bell-shaped curve. The central limit theorem doesn't hold in this case because

---

[1]https://www.r-project.org/

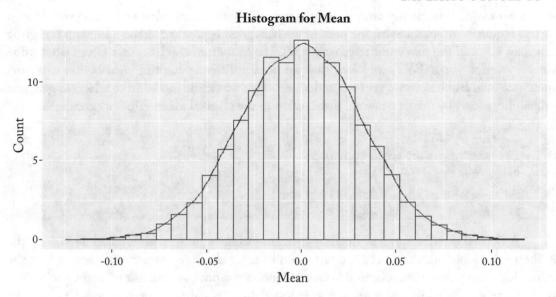

Figure 2.1: After sampling sets of 1,000 values from a standard normal distribution and computing the means over 10,000 trials, the histogram takes on the expected bell curve shape of a central tendency model, with a peak at 0.

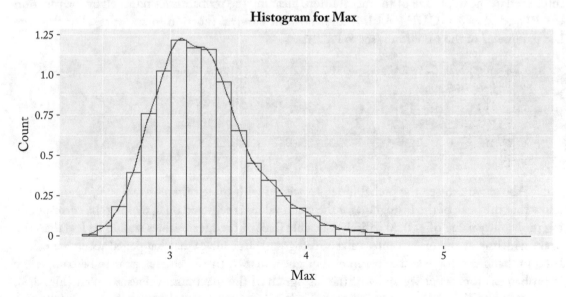

Figure 2.2: After repeating the same sampling procedure that underlies Fig. 2.1, but retaining the maximum values from each set of 1,000 values instead of computing the mean, the resulting histogram looks starkly different. The peak is now at 3.2, and there is noticeable skew.

we are no longer considering averages of a sampling from a distribution with finite variance—a formal requirement. Notice that the peak of the histogram is now at 3.2, the minimum is slightly less than 2.5, and the maximum approaches 5.0. The histogram also has skew. Given what we've already learned about EVT, we know that we need a different limiting distribution to model these maxima. But before we get to that, let's establish a baseline model from which to generate probability scores by fitting a normal distribution to the original mean values we computed:

```
library("MASS")
fitdistr(bufferMean, "normal")
#      mean             sd
# -0.0001344194 0.0313828480
# (0.0003138285) (0.0002219102)
```

A normal distribution is defined by two parameters: a mean and standard deviation. The R library MASS provides the fitdistr function in the code above, which was used to find the values for these parameters. Given this central tendency model, we can ask what the probability is for a variable s_i taking on a value that is less than or equal to a specified value point q by using the model's CDF. In this book, we will mainly concentrate on the output of measurable recognition functions, thus s_i will take the form of a score (distance or similarity). The function pnorm gives us access to the CDF via the two parameters we fit above. Let's assume that we are interested in the upper tail of the distribution, meaning the probabilities returned by the function are $P(s_i < q) = 1 - \text{CDF}$ (which is known as the survival function in statistics). For this, the last parameter of the function is set to FALSE.

```
pnorm(0, -0.0001344194, 0.0313828480, FALSE)
# [1] 0.4982913
pnorm(1, -0.0001344194, 0.0313828480, FALSE)
# [1] 3.611041e-223
pnorm(2, -0.0001344194, 0.0313828480, FALSE)
# [1] 0
```

Above we can see the probabilities associated with three different values: 0, 1, and 2. We know that the peak of the histogram for the mean values is centered on 0, making the corresponding probability value of ~ 0.50 entirely plausible (half of the mean values should be less than the peak, which is at the exact center of the histogram). But look what happened when we calculated probabilities for 1 and 2: based on our given model, these values appear to be completely improbable. From what we know of the histogram of the maximum values sampled (Fig. 2.2), it is not out of the realm of possibility that values less than about 4 can occur. To address this discrepancy, let's turn to an EVT distribution provided by the R library SpatialExtremes and assess the difference in the resulting probabilities. Fitting the Generalized Extreme Value (GEV) distribution over the maximum values we stored yields the following set of parameters:

```
library(SpatialExtremes)
gevmle(bufferMax)
    loc        scale        shape
3.08305916 0.29802546 -0.07158273
```

Note that instead of a mean and standard deviation, we now have three different parameters: location, scale, and shape. By invoking the GEV CDF via the pgev function, again using the upper tail of the distribution as a frame of reference, we can re-evaluate the values 0, 1 and 2. What appeared to be highly improbable with the central tendency model is now well within the realm of possibility:

```
pgev(0, 3.08305916, 0.29802546, -0.07158273, FALSE)
#[1] 1
pgev(1, 3.08305916, 0.29802546, -0.07158273, FALSE)
#[1] 1
pgev(2, 3.08305916, 0.29802546, -0.07158273, FALSE)
#[1] 1
pgev(3, 3.08305916, 0.29802546, -0.07158273, FALSE)
#[1] 0.7322732
pgev(4, 3.08305916, 0.29802546, -0.07158273, FALSE)
#[1] 0.03047941
```

Instead of having a probability of occurrence of 0, the values 1 and 2 are highly probable (recall that the peak of the histogram of maximums is at 3.2). Going beyond the initial set of values, the value 3 is also likely, and 4 possible, but very unlikely. By shifting the model's emphasis to the tail, we no longer underestimate values that have some plausible chance of occurring. The real-world implications of such a difference can be striking: the fields of hydrology (Smith [1986]), finance (Longin [2000]) and manufacturing (Castillo [1988]) all rely on EVT-based models to make accurate predictions of rare events.

2.2   THE EXTREME VALUE THEOREM

The example we just walked through highlighted the need for an alternative to the central limit theorem for modeling distributions of extremes, like the maxima above. For this, we can turn to the Fisher-Tippett Theorem (Fisher and Tippett [1928], Kotz and Nadarajah [2001]) also known as the first Extreme Value Theorem. Just as the central limit theorem indicates that the random variables generated from certain stochastic processes follow normal distributions, EVT indicates that given a well-behaved overall distribution of values (e.g., a distribution that is continuous and has an inverse), the distribution of the maximum or minimum values can assume only limited forms. To find the appropriate form, let us first define this theorem.

Theorem 2.2.1 *Let $(s_1, s_2, \ldots)$ be a sequence of i.i.d samples. Let $M_n = \max\{s_1, \ldots, s_n\}$. If a sequence of pairs of real numbers (a_n, b_n) exists such that each $a_n > 0$ and*

$$\lim_{x \to \infty} P\left(\frac{M_n - b_n}{a_n} \leq x\right) = F(x) \tag{2.2}$$

then if F is a non-degenerate distribution function, it belongs to one of three extreme value distributions: the Gumbel (I), Fréchet (II), or Reversed Weibull (III) distribution. Gumbel and Fréchet are for unbounded distributions and Reversed Weibull for bounded.

A special consideration must be made for modeling minima. Since the Fisher-Tippett Theorem applies to maxima, minima can be transformed to maxima via $z_i = -s_i$.

There are other types of extreme value theorems. While in this book we will mainly focus on models derived from the Fisher-Tippett Theorem, the second extreme value theorem, also known as the Pickands-Balkema-de Haan Theorem (Pickands [1975]), will come up from time to time—especially in the context of Pareto modeling. It addresses probabilities conditioned on the process exceeding a sufficiently high threshold. Consider an unknown distribution function F of a random sample s. The conditional excess distribution function F_u of the variable s above a threshold u is defined as:

$$F_u(x) = P(s - u \leq x | s > u) = \frac{F(u + x) - F(u)}{1 - F(u)} \tag{2.3}$$

for $0 \leq x \leq s_F - u$ where s_F is either the finite or infinite right endpoint of the underlying distribution F. F_u describes the distribution of the excess values over u. Given this definition, the Pickands-Balkema-de Haan Theorem can be stated.

Theorem 2.2.2 *Let $(s_1, s_2, \ldots)$ be a sequence of i.i.d. samples, and let F_u be their conditional excess distribution function. For a large class of underlying distribution functions F, and a large u, F_u is well approximated by the Generalized Pareto distribution:*

$$F_u(x) \to GPD_F(x), \text{ as } u \to \infty. \tag{2.4}$$

We will define the Generalized Pareto distribution GPD_F in the next section.

2.3   DISTRIBUTIONS IN THE EVT FAMILY

The Fisher-Tippett Theorem leads to three primary EVT distributions, and a number of other related distributions. In this section, we'll take a brief tour of the distributions that have some relevancy to visual recognition. In particular, the CDF of each distribution becomes significant in Chapters 4 and 5, where score normalization is used for fusion and supervised machine learning. Beyond the three primary extreme value distributions (Gumbel, Fréchet, and Reversed Weibull), the GEV, Rayleigh, and Pareto distributions are also useful for tail modeling. Recent work in computer vision has made use of these (Broadwater and Chellappa [2010], Fragoso and Turk [2013], Furon and Jégou [2013], Gibert et al. [2015a], Li et al. [2012], Scheirer et al. [2011], Shi et al. [2008]). For the following distributions, assume κ, λ, and τ are the shape, scale, and location parameters, respectively. The general process for many of the algorithms discussed in subsequent chapters will be to fit a particular model to the data to determine a defining set of parameters $\theta = \{\kappa, \lambda, \tau\}$. From θ, the CDF F can be used to make probabilistic predictions—the same exact process we described via code in Sec. 2.1.

2.3.1   GUMBEL DISTRIBUTION

The Gumbel is a distribution that applies when the data to be modeled are unbounded. It is used for modeling maxima (or minima, if the random variables are negated). Note that the shape of the Gumbel is not determined by the parameters—only the location and scale (which must be positive) are defined. The Probability Density Function (PDF) of the Gumbel distribution is given as:

$$GUMBEL_f(x) = \frac{1}{\lambda} e^{-(z + e^{-z})},$$ (2.5)

where

$$z = \frac{x - \tau}{\lambda}.$$ (2.6)

The CDF of the Gumbel distribution is given as:

$$GUMBEL_F(x) = e^{-e^{-(x-\tau)/\lambda}}.$$ (2.7)

Figure 2.3 shows the shape of the Gumbel distribution for three different sets of parameters. The Gumbel distribution has recently emerged in sampling strategies for machine learning through a technique called the Gumbel-Max trick. Sampling is necessary for training, evaluating and predicting probabilistic learning models. How to do this in a stable and efficient manner for a target distribution of interest is still an open question. The Gumbel-Max trick adds independent Gumbel perturbations to each configuration of a discrete negative energy function and returns the argmax configuration of the perturbed negative energy function. It can also lead to other formulations for continuous spaces (Maddison et al. [2014]).

2.3.2   FRÉCHET DISTRIBUTION

The Fréchet is a distribution that applies when the data to be modeled are bounded from below and a heavy upper tail is desirable. Like the Gumbel distribution, it is used for modeling maxima (or minima, if the random variables are negated). The PDF of the Fréchet distribution is given as:

$$FRECHET_f(x) = \frac{\kappa}{\lambda} \left(\frac{x - \tau}{\kappa}\right)^{-1-\kappa} e^{-\left(\frac{x-\tau}{\lambda}\right)^{\kappa}}.$$ (2.8)

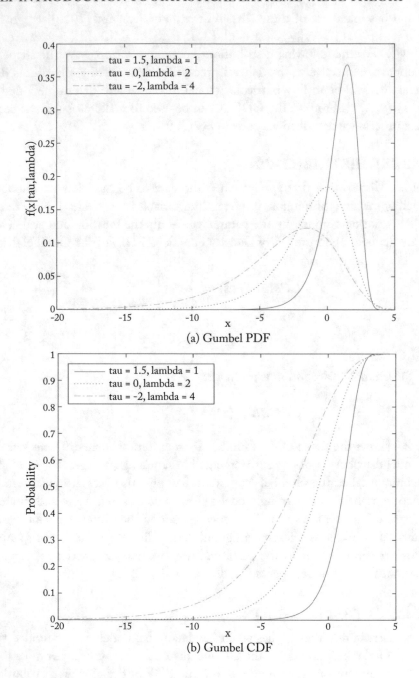

Figure 2.3: Gumbel PDFs and CDFs for three different sets of parameters.

The CDF of the Fréchet distribution is given as:

$$FRECHET_F(x) = e^{-\left(\frac{x-\tau}{\lambda}\right)^{-\kappa}}. \tag{2.9}$$

Figure 2.4 shows the shape of the Fréchet distribution for three different sets of parameters. Work thus far in computer vision and machine learning has avoided the Fréchet distribution for modeling maxima in favor of the more flexible reverse Weibull distribution, which need not have a heavy upper tail.

2.3.3   WEIBULL DISTRIBUTION

Weibull Distribution

The Weibull is a distribution that applies when the data to be modeled are bounded from below and the shape and scale parameters are positive. In contrast to the Gumbel and Fréchet distributions, the Weibull is used for modeling minima. The PDF of the two-parameter Weibull distribution is given as:

$$WEIBULL_f(x) = \begin{cases} \frac{\kappa}{\lambda}\left(\frac{x}{\lambda}\right)^{\kappa-1} e^{-(x/\lambda)^\kappa} & x \geq 0 \\ 0 & x < 0. \end{cases} \tag{2.10}$$

The CDF of the Weibull distribution is given as:

$$WEIBULL_F(x) = \begin{cases} 1 - e^{-(x/\lambda)^\kappa} & x \geq 0 \\ 0 & x < 0. \end{cases} \tag{2.11}$$

Figure 2.5 shows the shape of the Weibull distribution for three different sets of parameters.

Reverse Weibull Distribution

The reverse Weibull distribution is simply the opposite of the Weibull's non-degenerate distribution function, and is appropriate when the data are bounded from above. It follows directly from the Fisher-Tippett Theorem, and is thus used to model maxima.

$$RWEIBULL_F(x) = \begin{cases} e^{-(x/\lambda)^\kappa} & x < 0 \\ 1 & x \geq 0. \end{cases} \tag{2.12}$$

Both the Weibull and Reverse Weibull have been applied to various visual recognition problems in computer vision (Scheirer et al. [2010, 2011, 2012a, 2014a]). We will make extensive use of these distributions in Chapters 3–5.

2.3.4   GENERALIZED EXTREME VALUE DISTRIBUTION

The Generalized Extreme Value Distribution (GEV) is a generalization of the Gumbel, Fréchet and reverse Weibull distributions (all three are maximum EVT distributions). The PDF of the

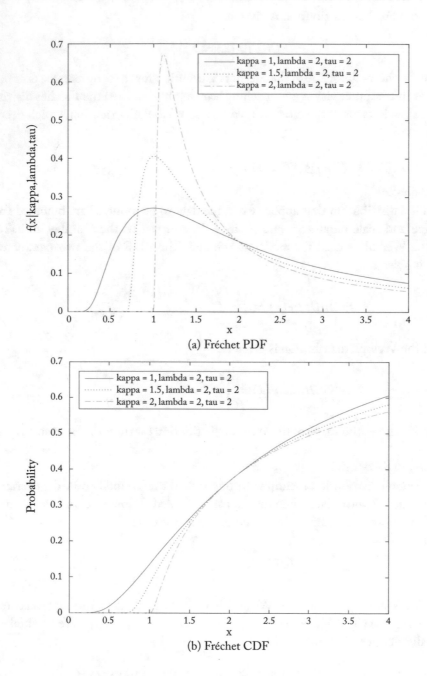

(a) Fréchet PDF

(b) Fréchet CDF

Figure 2.4: Fréchet PDFs and CDFs for three different sets of parameters.

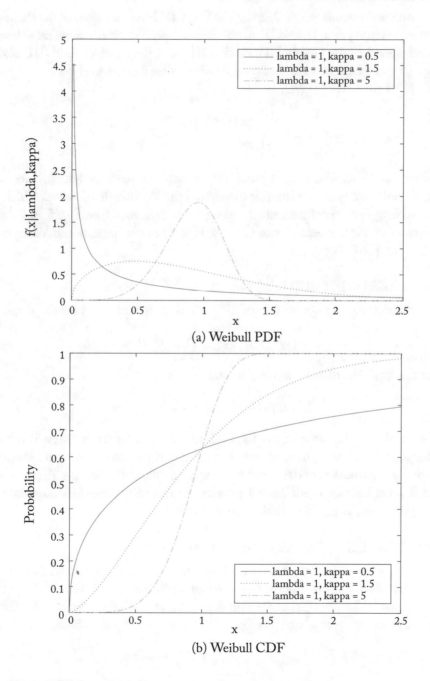

(a) Weibull PDF

(b) Weibull CDF

Figure 2.5: Weibull PDFs and CDFs for three different sets of parameters.

GEV distribution was introduced in Chapter 1 as Eq. 1.1. Different values of the shape parameter yield the extreme value type I, II, and III distributions. Specifically, the three cases $\kappa = 0, \kappa > 0$, and $\kappa < 0$ correspond to the Gumbel (I), Frechet (II), and Reversed Weibull (III) distributions. Thus the sign of κ can be used as an indicator of which distribution to choose.

The CDF of the GEV is given as:

$$GEV_F(x) = \begin{cases} e^{-\left(1+\left(\frac{x-\tau}{\lambda}\right)\kappa\right)^{-1/\kappa}} & \text{if } \kappa \neq 0 \\ e^{-e^{-(x-\tau)/\lambda}} & \text{if } \kappa = 0. \end{cases} \tag{2.13}$$

The GEV can be applied to the task of post-recognition score analysis (the focus of Chapter 3), but the results are generally inferior to those of the Weibull distribution, which is a better match for modeling data from measurable recognition functions (see Fig. 5 in Scheirer et al. [2011]). Nevertheless, it has been successfully used for score normalization in unsupervised data clustering (Li et al. [2012]).

2.3.5 RAYLEIGH DISTRIBUTION

The Rayleigh distribution is a special case of the Weibull distribution, where the shape parameter $\kappa = 2$.

$$RAYLEIGH_f(x) = \frac{x}{\lambda^2} e^{-x^2/2\lambda^2}. \tag{2.14}$$

The CDF of the Rayleigh distribution is given as:

$$RAYLEIGH_F(x) = 1 - e^{-x^2/2\lambda^2}. \tag{2.15}$$

Figure 2.6 shows the shape of the Rayleigh distribution for three different sets of parameters. Fragoso and Turk [2013] have argued that the Rayleigh distribution can reduce sensitivity to the underlying distribution of data, and be computed efficiently, because the scale is the only parameter that must be computed. They demonstrated its utility for guided sampling for image feature correspondence, which we will discuss further in Chapter 3.

2.3.6 GENERALIZED PARETO DISTRIBUTION

The Generalized Pareto Distribution (GPD) is a common distribution used to model the tails drawn from other distributions. As we discussed above in Sec. 2.2, it follows from the second extreme value theorem (i.e., the Pickands-Balkema-de Haan Theorem). Specifically, the modeling accounts for exceedances over a high threshold ($x - t$, where t is a threshold).

$$GPD_f(x) = \frac{1}{\lambda}(1 + \kappa z)^{-(1/\kappa+1)}, \tag{2.16}$$

where

$$z = \frac{x - \tau}{\lambda}. \tag{2.17}$$

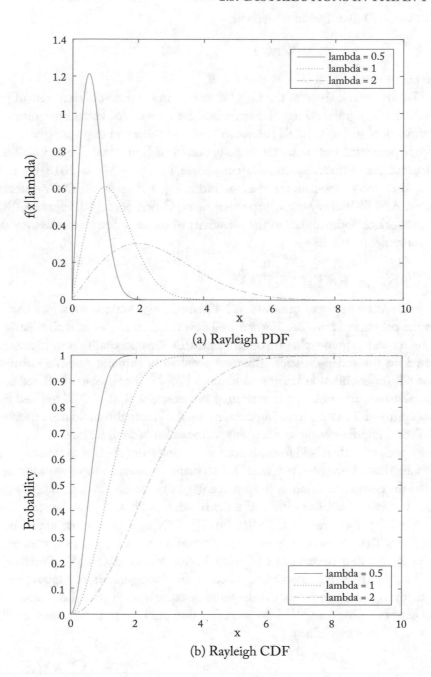

(a) Rayleigh PDF

(b) Rayleigh CDF

Figure 2.6: Rayleigh PDFs and CDFs for three different sets of parameters.

The CDF of the GPD distribution is given as:

$$GPD_F(x) = 1 - (1 + \kappa z)^{(-1/\kappa)} \tag{2.18}$$

for the three parameters: $k \in \mathbb{R}$, $\lambda > 0$, and $\tau \in \mathbb{R}$.

Figure 2.7 shows the shape of the GPD distribution for three different sets of parameters. The GPD has been a popular choice of distribution for a variety of visual recognition tasks. For biometric verification, Shi et al. [2008] chose to model genuine and impostor distributions using the GPD. For hyperspectral and radar target detection, Broadwater and Chellappa [2010] applied GPD to isolate extrema within a potential target sample. Furon and Jégou [2013] argue that image retrieval is another good candidate for extrema modeling, and apply GPD for outlier detection in that context. And for railway track inspection tasks, Gibert et al. [2015a] use GPD within a Bayesian framework to optimally adjust the sensitivity of anomaly detectors. We look at these last two cases in more detail in Chapter 4.

2.4   TAIL SIZE ESTIMATION

Tail size estimation is a key open question in EVT modeling. Various strategies have been proposed, from the principled to *ad hoc*. Several well developed strategies exist for distributions derived from the second extreme value theorem like GPD. One possibility is to measure empirical quantiles based on the order statistics. The dual problem of extreme quantile estimation is the estimation of tail probability (de Haan and Ferreira [2007]). For problems related to modeling the score distributions from biometric matching systems, Shi et al. [2008] applied the quintile measurement approach to a set of training data, where the Pareto threshold can be varied to assess the quality of resulting distributional fits over specific estimated tail regions.

For non-peak over threshold formulations stemming from the first extreme value theorem, various *ad hoc* methods have been proposed for specialized cases. In most approaches that have been proposed for computer vision, a fixed percentage of data points (e.g., 5%, 10%, 25%) not exceeding the maximum tail size (50%) of a distribution is chosen (Fragoso and Turk [2013], Gibert et al. [2015a], Scheirer et al. [2010, 2011]). This applies in some approximation, but essentially reduces the problem of parameter estimation to setting a free parameter. When considering problems that make use of Support Vector Machines (SVM), a method proposed by Jain et al. [2014] can make an estimate based on the configuration of support vectors in the model. The method considers points within some distance ϵ of the SVM decision boundary as the potential extrema. Given an SVM decision function $h(x)$, an indicator function B^+ and the positive tail size T_ϵ^+ can be defined:

$$B^+(x; \epsilon) = \begin{cases} 1 & \text{if } h(x) \leq \epsilon \\ 0 & \text{otherwise} \end{cases} \qquad \text{and} \qquad T_\epsilon^+ = \sum_{x \in \mathcal{M}_y} B^+(x; \epsilon), \tag{2.19}$$

where $\mathcal{M}_y$ is the set of positive points associated with class y. For a soft margin Radial Basis Function (RBF) SVM, support vectors include all points on or outside the positive-class region

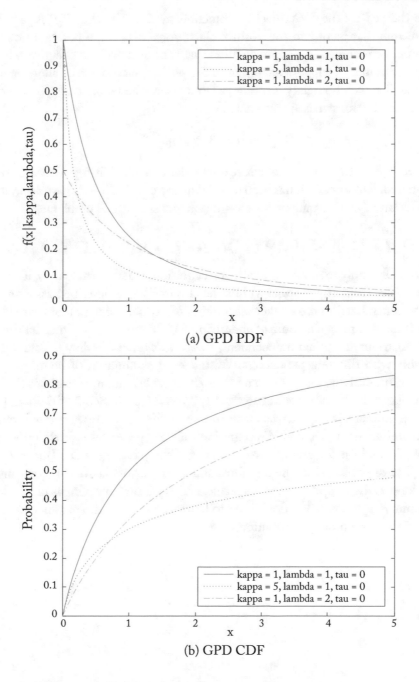

(a) GPD PDF

(b) GPD CDF

Figure 2.7: GPD PDFs and CDFs for three different sets of parameters.

boundary as defined by the SVM decision function in Eq. 5.2. Thus T_0^+ is just the number of support vectors that belong to the positive class. For $\epsilon > 0$, some points inside the positive boundary would be included. An approximation that is both stable and effective is to use a small multiple of the number of support vectors from the positive class, thereby allowing a few points inside but near the class boundary. Letting $|\alpha^+|$ represent the number of support vectors from the positive class, the tail size is approximated via:

$$\hat{T}_\epsilon^+ = \max(3, \psi \times |\alpha^+|), \qquad (2.20)$$

where we need ≥ 3 distinct points to ensure a well-defined EVT fitting. One free parameter ψ must be estimated. Empirically, it has been found that any $\psi \in [1.25 - 2.5]$ works well. This range has provided relatively stable multi-class recognition across multiple problems.

2.5   THE I.I.D. ASSUMPTION AND VISUAL DATA

Does EVT actually apply to problems in visual recognition, where we are rarely, if ever, presented with i.i.d. variables from any process? While the classic EVT is described assuming i.i.d. samples, it can be generalized to the weaker assumption of exchangeable random variables (Berman [1962]), resulting in at most a mixture of underlying EVT distributions. Consider the special case of identically distributed, but not independent, *exchangeable variables* drawn from the same EVT family, possibly with different parameters. With a mild assumption of bounded mean-square convergence, the underlying distribution under exchangeable random variables is the same distribution as the classic EVT case (see Theorems 2.1, 2.2 and Corollary 2.2 of Berman [1962]). For the recognition problem, it is quite reasonable to assume that the scores generated from matching one class vs. another via a measurable recognition function generates a distribution with a form that does not depend on the classes involved, even if the parameters do. This is a rather weak assumption. The distribution can be any form and each pair of classes can have any set of parameters, as long as the sampling is exchangeable, i.e., any future sampling is predicable based on the past sampling experience. We don't need to know the form or the parameters, we just must assume it exists and is a proper distribution.

CHAPTER 3

Post-recognition Score Analysis

Thus far, we've mostly discussed EVT in the context of distributions with abstract relationships to visual data. In order to make the transition from theory to practice, we will assume that scores are available as samples drawn from some distribution reflecting the output of a measurable recognition function. The distance or similarity score produced by a recognition function (e.g., a distance calculation between two vectors or a machine learning-based model) is a primary artifact of the pattern recognition process itself, and can tell us much about specific instances of visual perception. Most typically in automatic visual recognition, little, if anything, is currently done with these scores beyond checking the sign to assign class membership, or perhaps a quick comparison against an *ad hoc* threshold to accept or reject a sample. At a fundamental level, we can ask what exactly a recognition score is and why it is important for decision making. Further, we can model distributions of scores to determine if they were generated by a matching or non-matching process. Once we understand this basic model, we can then extend it to other modes such as score normalization and calibration (see Chapters 4 and 5). In this chapter, we will examine the problem of failure prediction as a case study embodying these concepts.

3.1 FAILURE PREDICTION FOR RECOGNITION SYSTEMS

In computer vision, the ability to assess the *quality* of an image (Wang et al. [2004]) before submitting it to feature extraction and a subsequent recognition algorithm remains a tantalizing possibility. While rarely applied to object classification or detection tasks, image quality assessment is a mainstay of biometric systems, where it is believed to improve the overall reliability of matching (Grother and Tabassi [2007], Tabassi et al. [2004]). This is a form of *failure prediction*, the ability to automatically determine whether or not the decision of a recognition system can be trusted as a true match or non-match. Failure prediction is distinct from the typical consideration of a matching decision via an empirically derived threshold, in that it is meant to signal that something has gone wrong with the recognition instance under consideration—even if a matching threshold was exceeded. Returning to image quality, it is in some sense intuitive that images of poor visual appearance should match poorly to any stored representations in a database—after all, if we as humans judge an image to be highly impacted by artifacts, it seems to follow naturally that an algorithm will struggle to match it correctly.

Or so we think: the biometrics literature provides some counter-intuitive evidence that brings the entire assumption of image quality as a useful predictor of algorithm failure into question. For the Face Recognition Vendor Test (FRVT), a National Institute of Standards and Technology (NIST) run assessment of commercial face recognition algorithms, Beveridge et al. [2008] found that while quality is a reasonable predictor of algorithm performance overall, it can vary drastically as a function of the co-variates (e.g., focus, face size, or environment) on a per-image basis. Similarly, in the analysis that followed the Iris Challenge Evaluation (ICE), a NIST run assessment of commercial iris recognition algorithms, Flynn [2008] found that three iris image quality assessment algorithms lacked correlation. This suggests that each algorithm was measuring different aspects of quality, or measuring the same aspects of quality, but at different degrees of accuracy. In either case, we can conclude that there are lingering questions related to what the term quality even means, as well as how it should be assessed.

At a fundamental level, we can question the assumption that making any prediction about the performance of a recognition system based entirely on the input is an effective strategy. Phillips and Beveridge [2009] introduced the theory of "biometric completeness," which states that a perfect quality measure for any algorithm would be equivalent to finding a perfect matching algorithm. Thus, we could simply eschew the use of a recognition algorithm and use the quality assessment algorithm in its place. While originally proposed for biometrics, the essence of this completeness theory applies to any recognition system making use of an image quality assessment component. This provides some practical framing of the limits of quality assessment as a practice, and redirects our attention to the *scores* coming out of any algorithm that makes a prediction. To quote Beveridge [2008], "Quality is not in the eye of the beholder; *it is in the recognition performance figures!*"

Taking the above quotation to heart, an alternative to predicting failures from image quality assessment is to apply machine learning over features derived from the scores of the recognition algorithm (Li et al. [2005], Riopka and Boult [2005], Scheirer and Boult [2008], Scheirer et al. [2008, 2012b], Wang et al. [2007]). The raw scores are not useful by themselves as features, but transformations that have a normalizing effect over the raw scores s_i, coupled with the benefit of learning over many examples, facilitate the training of accurate failure prediction models (Scheirer et al. [2012b]). Specifically, delta features between scores ($\Delta_{i,j...k} = \langle (s_i - s_j), (s_i - s_{j+1}), ..., (s_i - s_k) \rangle$, where $j = i + 1$) or Discrete Cosine Transform (DCT) features can be computed. Training then takes place over matching and non-matching instances of feature vectors composed of these feature sets. Common supervised classification approaches such as boosting (Li et al. [2005]), neural networks (Riopka and Boult [2005]), and SVM (Scheirer and Boult [2008], Scheirer et al. [2008]) have been shown to be effective for failure prediction.

Yet another way to predict failure is to train classifiers on features that describe the failure modes for particular vision applications such as semantic segmentation, vanishing point and camera parameter estimation, and image memorability prediction. The methodology described by Zhang et al. [2014] does this via the analysis of image-level features from the input. In a sense, this is a form of image quality assessment that goes beyond metrics of overall image clarity to quantify conditions that are known to impact specific applications. While low-level features are to some extent effective, more can be done to characterize failure modes through a semantic

reasoning process. Bansal et al. [2014] suggest generating a "specification sheet" composed of se-
mantically meaningful image attributes that may or may not be present under conditions where
vision applications fail (for example: "If the test image is blurry, or the face is not frontal, or the
person to be recognized is a young white woman with heavy make up, the system is likely to
fail."). These attributes can be computed automatically via trained classifiers. For face and object
recognition, this approach has been shown to be a useful predictor. However, individual specification sheets must be changed every time the application and/or image domain change—even if
the same underlying recognition algorithm is used.

Extending some of the aforementioned ideas with deep learning, Daftry et al. [2016] introduce the notion of *introspection*, which is a learned model of the performance characteristics
of the underlying recognition algorithm. To implement this, a multi-step supervised learning algorithm is deployed. For feature extraction, a deep spatio-temporal convolutional neural network
is trained to learn good invariant hidden latent representations of target algorithm performance.
Features are extracted from this model and used as input to a linear SVM, which produces predictions of failure as output. A data-driven approach is certainly viable for failure prediction, but
like all learning problems, this form of model introspection is prone to overfitting and thus lack
of generalization across trials.

Is there a better way to do this? Failure prediction from machine learning is, in some sense,
ad hoc—constrained by the need to constantly retrain for new recognition circumstances. Ideally,
failure prediction should proceed on a per instance matching basis without any need for supervised
pre-training. Through the use of statistical models fit to the distribution of scores generated during
a particular matching instance, this turns out to be possible. Moreover, if we assume that there is
some importance assigned to the scores in the tail of that distribution, based on the knowledge
that matches should receive high scores (or low scores, if considering a distance function), then
we can invoke the EVT. An EVT model will allow us to make good predictions about failures
in a recognition system via statistical hypothesis testing. This is a paradigm that is called *meta-
recognition* (Scheirer et al. [2011]).

3.2   META-RECOGNITION

Meta-recognition draws its inspiration from observations about decision making in biological
systems. In psychology, the term *meta-cognition* refers to "knowing about knowing" (Flavell and
Wellman [1988]). To wit, the human mind has knowledge of its own cognitive processes, and
can use it to develop strategies to improve cognitive performance. For example, if a student no-
tices that he has more trouble learning Spanish than probability theory, he "knows" something
about his learning ability and can take corrective action to improve his academic performance. At
an even deeper level, processes within the brain itself exhibit a similar phenomenon. Eshel et al.
[2013] report that dopamine neurons promote learning by signaling prediction errors, the difference between actual and expected outcomes for a behavioral task. This primitive form of failure
prediction allows for efficient adaptive learning at the cellular level, yet still conforms to the basic

model of "knowing about knowing." The standard definition of meta-cognition (Cox [2005]) can be adapted to define meta-recognition, which applies specifically to recognition algorithms, in a formal sense:

Definition 3.2.1 *Let* X *be a recognition system. We define* Y *to be a* meta-recognition *system when recognition state information flows from* X *to* Y*, control information flows from* Y *to* X*, and* Y *analyzes the recognition performance of* X*, adjusting the control information based upon the observations.*

The relationship between X and Y can be seen in Fig. 3.1, where Y is labeled "Meta-Recognition System." Y can be any approximation of the cognitive process, including an artificial neural network (Riopka and Boult [2005]), SVM (Scheirer et al. [2008]), or statistical method (Scheirer et al. [2011]). For score-based meta-recognition, the primary approach considered in this chapter, Y observes the recognition scores produced by X, and if necessary, adjusts the recognition decisions and perhaps signals for a specific response action.

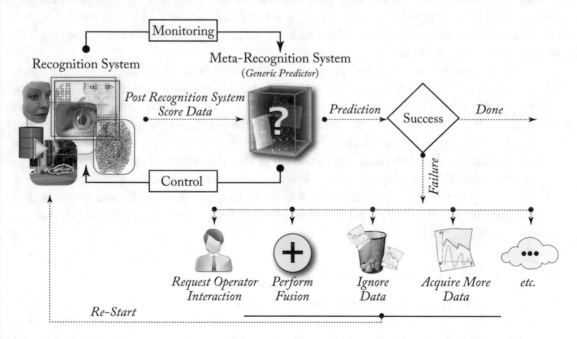

Figure 3.1: An overview of the meta-recognition process for post-recognition score analysis, facilitating failure prediction. Recognition systems can be any process that makes a decision about a vector x in some multidimensional feature space $\mathbb{R}^d$. Based upon the scores produced by some recognition system for a single input x, a prediction of success or failure is made by the meta-recognition system. Based on these predictions, action can be taken to improve the overall accuracy of the recognition system. From Scheirer et al. [2011].

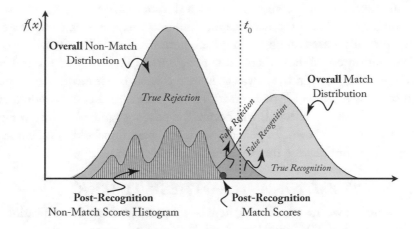

Figure 3.2: The match and non-match distributions for the recognition problem (based on Scheirer et al. [2011]). A threshold t_0 applied to the score determines the decision for recognition or rejection. Where the tails of the two distributions overlap is where we find *False Rejections* and *False Recognition*. Embedded within the overall distribution is a particular set of post-recognition scores, with one match (falsely rejected by the threshold t_0) and many non-match samples. Based on Scheirer et al. [2011] .

3.2.1 A FORMAL MODEL OF RECOGNITION

To begin developing a framework for meta-recognition, let's attempt to understand what a recognition score s from some recognition system $f(x)$ actually is. Consider the general definition of Shakhnarovich et al. [2002], where the task of a recognition system is to find the class label y^*, where p_k is an underlying probability rule and p_0 is the input distribution, satisfying

$$y^* = \operatorname*{argmax}_{class\ y} Pr(p_0 = p_y) \tag{3.1}$$

subject to $Pr(p_0 = p_{y^*}) \geq 1 - \delta$ for a given confidence threshold δ, or to conclude the lack of such a class (to reject the input). The test sample is the input image p_0 submitted to the system with its corresponding class label y^*. The overall recognition model is all the classes y^* known to the recognition system. We call this rank-1 recognition (a term borrowed from the biometrics literature) because if we sort the class probabilities, the recognition is based on the highest value. One can generalize the concept of recognition, as is common in image search and some biometrics problems, by relaxing the requirement for success to having the correct answer in the top K responses. For analysis, assuming the ground-truth is known, one can define the overall match and non-match distributions for recognition and the per-instance post-recognition distributions (see Fig. 3.2).

Many systems replace the probability in the above definition with a more generic "score," for which argmax produces the same answer when the posterior class probability is monotonic with the score function. For an operational system, a threshold t_0 on the similarity score s is set to define the boundary between proposed matches and proposed non-matches. The choice of t_0 is often made empirically, based on observed system performance. Where t_0 falls on each tail of each overall distribution establishes where *False Recognition* (Type I error: the test image does not have a corresponding entry in the model of known classes, but is incorrectly associated with a gallery entry) or *False Rejection* (Type II error: the test image has a corresponding entry in the model of known classes, but is rejected) will occur. The post-recognition scores in Fig. 3.2 yield a False Rejection for the t_0 shown. In general, setting a fixed threshold t_0 on similarity scores produces a recognition confidence δ that varies with each test sample.

3.2.2 META-RECOGNITION AS HYPOTHESIS TESTING

The mode of recognition we are considering here is not pair matching or verification, which are 1:1 matching scenarios, but 1:N matching where N is typically a reasonably large sampling of different classes (for a full discussion and formalization of recognition modes, see Scheirer et al. [2014b]). This is the most common matching scenario for visual object recognition (e.g., the ImageNet Visual Recognition Challenge protocols defined by Russakovsky et al. [2015]), and it also applies to more specialized forms of visual recognition like biometric identification. For a correct match, we will have $N - 1$ non-matching scores to consider—not enough to build a model for the match distribution.

Because each recognition instance produces many non-match scores, the meta-recognition problem can instead be formalized as determining if the top K scores contain an outlier with respect to the current test image's non-match distribution. In particular, let $\mathcal{F}(p)$ be the distribution of the non-match scores that are generated by matching against the test image p, and $m(p)$ to be the match score for that test image. In addition, let $S(K) = s_1 \ldots s_K$ be the top K sorted scores. We can formalize the null hypothesis H_0 of our prediction for rank-K recognition as:

$$H_0 \ (failure) : \forall x \in S(K), x \in \mathcal{F}(p). \tag{3.2}$$

If we can reject H_0 (*failure*), then we predict success. So far, so good. But we require a statistical model in order to apply this test.

3.2.3 WEIBULL-BASED META-RECOGNITION

We noted above that meta-recognition leads to an extreme value problem. But why, in a theoretical sense, is this the case? After all, it is possible to fit a Gaussian distribution to the score data and make predictions based on the resulting model. Part of the answer is that we're not interested in the entire score distribution, but instead in the top K scores that are potential candidates for a valid recognition result. This leads to a tail modeling problem, where only a limited number of distributions apply (see Sec. 2.3). The application of EVT to computer vision is a recent development. Thus, we turn to the finance literature, where EVT as a tool of analysis has been commonplace for many years, for a suitable framing to the problem.

In the business world, assets and investments are collected in portfolios, which are owned by an individual or institution, and managed by the owner or an outside professional when the amount of money involved is substantially large. Portfolio management is the practice of maximizing the returns on the portfolio while managing risk. A great deal of risk assessment that takes place these days in finance is based on statistical modeling, which attempts to account for market movements—including rare events—that will trigger a reduction in value. However, a significant burden is placed on the data scientist performing the analysis—does the model reflect accurate probabilities about rare events occurring? As we saw in Sec. 2.1, central tendency modeling can grossly underestimate the probability of a rare event having a serious impact. Thus, EVT models are used in finance to assess the impact of market crashes or other situations of extreme stress on investment portfolios (Bensalah [2000]). A collection of portfolios will yield extrema that are underpinned by these fluctuations, making it possible to fit a distribution across the collection. For example, one can imagine a geographically confined financial crisis impacting relatively few assets within a portfolio. But some assets will be affected in a drastic way, depressing prices across portfolios. EVT is the correct model to apply to the distribution of extrema from each portfolio in this scenario.

To see that recognition in computer vision is an extreme value problem in a formal sense, we can consider the recognition problem as logically starting with a collection of portfolios (in analogy to EVT modeling in finance). Each portfolio is an independent subset of the gallery or recognition classes. This is shown in Fig. 3.3. From each portfolio, we can compute the "best" matching score in that portfolio. We can then collect a subset of all the scores that are maxima (extrema) within their respective portfolios. The tail of the post-match distribution of scores will be the best scores from the best of the portfolios. Thus modeling the non-match data in the tail is indeed an extreme value problem.

A particular portfolio is represented as the sampling $(s_1, s_2, \ldots)$ drawn from an overall distribution of scores S. The maximum of a portfolio is a single sample from the distribution function $F(x)$. Theorem 2.2.1 tells us that a large set of individual maxima M_n from the portfolios must converge to an extreme value distribution. As portfolio maxima fall into the tail of S, they can be most accurately modeled by the appropriate extreme value distribution. The assumptions necessary to apply this for a recognition problem are that we have sufficiently many classes for the portfolio model to be good enough for the approximation in the limit to apply, and that the portfolio samples are i.i.d. (see the discussion of the relaxation of this constraint in Chapter 2).

Given these observations, an algorithm can be developed that will let us apply Eq. 3.2. First, we must determine which distribution to use to fit the statistical model. If we assume that the match scores are bounded, then the distribution of the minimum (or maximum) reduces to a Weibull (or Reversed Weibull), independent of the choice of model for the individual non-match distribution (National Institute of Standards and Technology [2012]). For most recognition systems, the distance or similarity scores are bounded from below or above. If the values are unbounded, the GEV distribution can be used, though this is an uncommon scenario for visual

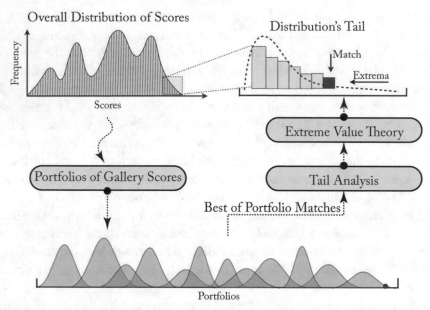

Figure 3.3: Why meta-recognition is an extreme value problem (based on Scheirer et al. [2011]). Consider a collection of portfolios composed of subsets of the gallery, each of which produces scores. One portfolio contains a match-score (red), the rest are non-matching scores (brown). The best of the best of the portfolio scores are those that show up in the tail of the post-recognition score distribution— leaving us with an extreme value problem. The best score in the tail is, if a match, an outlier with respect to the EVT model of the non-match data. Based on Scheirer et al. [2011].

recognition problems where distance or similarity measures predominate. Most importantly, we don't have to assume distributional models for the match or non-match distributions. Rephrasing, no matter what model best fits each overall non-match distribution, with enough samples and enough classes, the sampling of the top-K scores always results in a EVT distribution, and is a form of the Weibull if the data are bounded.

Given the potential variations that can occur in the class for which the test image belongs, there is a distribution of scores that occurs for each of the classes within the model. Figure 3.3 depicts the recognition of a given test image as implicitly sampling from these distributions. The algorithm, detailed in Alg. 3.1, takes the tail of these scores, which are likely to have been sampled from the extrema of their underlying portfolios, and fits a Reverse Weibull or Weibull distribution to that data, depending on the way the scores are bounded. Given the model's fit to the data, the meta-recognition process proceeds by using the hypothesis test of Eq. 3.2 to determine if the top score is an outlier by determining the probability of failure directly from the inverse CDF of that matching instance.

For Alg. 3.1 to be applied successfully, a couple of considerations must be made. First, there is the question of tail size. In practice, we do not know exactly where the sequence of extrema terminates. However, we have a few options that can help us estimate the tail size: cross validation over a known training data set that leads to a useful set of parameters for the model, tail probability estimation via Maximum Likelihood Estimators, and tail probability estimation via Moment Estimators (see Chapter 2 and de Haan and Ferreira [2007] for options related to these approaches and others). Second, there is the choice of the significance level threshold δ needed for the hypothesis test. If the top score s_1 exceeds the value of the inverse CDF of δ, then the failure prediction hypothesis can be rejected, yielding a prediction of success. Empirically, a very large δ has been found to work well, e.g., $\delta = 1 - 10^{-8}$. Note that meta-recognition is distinct from *ad hoc* score thresholding, as well as thresholding based on the scale and shape parameters of the Reverse Weibull or Weibull distributions, which do not reflect failure in any meaningful way (see Fig. 3.4).

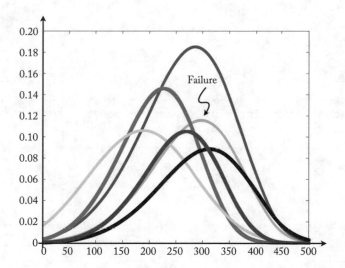

Figure 3.4: Weibull distributions recovered from six different real-matches (from the finger LI set of the NIST BSSR1 multibiometric data set (National Institute of Standards and Technology [2004])), one is a failure (not rank-1 recognition), five are successes. Per-instance success and failure distributions are not distinguishable by shape or position. In this example, the green distribution is a recognition failure, while the rest are successes. Based on Scheirer et al. [2011].

libMR (`https://github.com/Vastlab/libMR`) is a C++ library that provides meta-recognition and statistical EVT fitting functionality supporting a practical implementation of Alg. 3.1. It uses Maximum Likelihood Estimation (MLE) to find the location, scale and shape parameters that best fit a sequence of scores, and provides further functionality for failure prediction based on the resulting models. After installing and building the library, code can be written

---

Algorithm 3.1 Rank-1 statistical meta-recognition.

Require: A collection of similarity scores S; hypothesis test significance level threshold δ.

1: **Sort** and retain the n best (largest or smallest) scores, $s_1, \ldots, s_n \in S$;
2: **Fit** a Reverse Weibull or Weibull distribution W to $s_2, \ldots, s_n$, skipping the hypothesized outlier;
3: **if** $Inv(\delta; W) < s_1$ **then**
4:   s_1 is an outlier and we reject the failure prediction (null) hypothesis H_0.
5: **end if**

---

that takes advantage of these features. Let's look at a simple example for a sequence of 10 recognition scores representing the tail of an overall score distribution:

```c
#include <stdio.h>
#include "libMR/MetaRecognition.h"

int main(int argc, char **argv)
{
  double tail[] = {0.25419999999999998, 0.32952, 0.34912, 0.35493,
  0.35500, 0.35598, 0.35705, 0.35721, 0.35756, 0.35921};
  int length = sizeof(tail) / sizeof(double);

  MetaRecognition mr(true);
  mr.FitLow(tail, length);
  mr.Save((char*) "mr.txt");
  for (int i = 0; i < length; i++)
  {
   bool predict = mr.Predict_Match(tail[i]);
   if (predict)
    printf("%d:success ", i);
   else
    printf("%d:failure ", i);
  }
  printf("\n");
}
```

Assume here that the scores are distances (lower scores are better), and that the score 0.25419999999999998 represents a true match for the matching instance it came from. Three library functions support the meta-recognition process. First, a `MetaRecognition` object `mr` is instantiated with the option "true," meaning the hypothesized outlier (i.e., the lowest score) is skipped during fitting. Next, a Weibull distribution is fit to nine scores via the `FitLow()` function; parameters are stored within the mr object. Finally, predictions are made for all ten scores via the `Predict_Match()` function. One additional function, `Save()` is called to preserve the model on disk so that it can be used in the future without recomputing the fitting.

To compile this code, first copy the above self-contained program to the library directory `libMR/examples` as `mr-test.cpp`. Then run `make` from the `libMR/build/examples` directory. After `mr-test` is executed, the following output should be observed:

```
$ ./mr-test
0:success 1:failure 2:failure 3:failure 4:failure 5:failure 6:failure
7:failure 8:failure 9:failure
```

As expected, the first score is predicted to be a successful match, whereas the remaining scores are all predicted to be failures. This process was accomplished in an entirely training-free manner, making it a convenient tool for failure prediction across the board in computer vision. libMR provides a number of other functions for score transformations and normalization, which are described in the library's documentation. We will look at another feature of this library, w-score normalization, in the next chapter.

3.2.4   VALIDATION TOOLS FOR META-RECOGNITION

In order to assess the performance of meta-recognition for failure prediction, an analysis tool similar to a detection error trade-off curve (Martin et al. [1997]) is required, which allows us to vary parameters to gain a broad overview of the system behavior. Instead of using the familiar terminology of false positive rate and false negative rate for the axes, we will recast the errors in the context of making a prediction about a rank-1 recognition score. The underlying recognition system has its own error rate, which could be assessed via a cumulative match curve or a summary statistic—but such information is not necessary for our assessment of the meta-recognition prediction performance. A "Meta-Recognition Error Trade-off Curve" (MRET) is calculated from the following four cases.

C_1 **"False Accept,"** when meta-recognition predicts that the recognition system will succeed but the rank-1 score is not correct.

C_2 **"False Reject,"** when meta-recognition predicts that the recognition system will fail but the rank-1 score is correct.

C_3 **"True Accept,"** when both the recognition system and meta-recognition indicate a successful match.

C_4 **"True Reject,"** when meta-recognition predicts correctly that the underlying recognition system is failing.

The Meta-Recognition False Accept Rate (MRFAR) is the rate at which meta-recognition incorrectly predicts success, and the Meta-Recognition Miss Detection Rate (MRMDR) is the

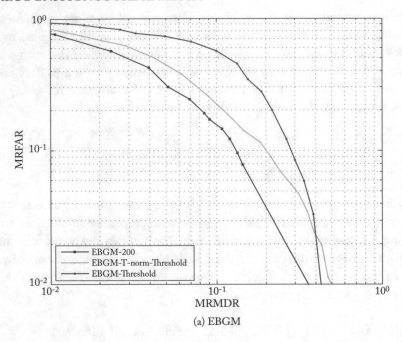

(a) EBGM

Figure 3.5: MRET curves for the EBGM face recognition algorithm (Okada et al. [1998]) on the FERET dataset (Scheirer et al. [2011]) and BSSR1 (National Institute of Standards and Technology [2004]), NIST's multibiometric data set incorporating scores from two face recognition algorithms and one fingerprint recognition algorithm operating over two different fingers. (a) shows meta-recognition predictions, along with predictions from two other simpler thresholding schemes for comparison. Meta-recognition is a better predictor in this case. Based on Scheirer et al. [2011]. *(Continues.)*

rate at which the meta-recognition incorrectly predicts failure. These error rates are formally defined as:

$$MRFAR = \frac{|C_1|}{|C_1| + |C_4|}, \quad MRMDR = \frac{|C_2|}{|C_2| + |C_3|}. \tag{3.3}$$

Both are a convenient indication of meta-recognition performance. The MRFAR and MRMDR can be adjusted via thresholding applied to the predictions to build a curve. Just as one uses a traditional DET or ROC curve to set verification system parameters, the meta-recognition parameters can be tuned using the MRET. MRET curves for the EBGM face recognition algorithm (Okada et al. [1998], Scheirer et al. [2011]) and NIST's multibiometric score set (National Institute of Standards and Technology [2004]) are shown in Fig. 3.5. To interpret these plots, it should be understood that points approaching the lower lefthand corner minimize both the MRFAR and MRMDR errors. The MRET is not specific to meta-recognition, and can help us understand the performance differences between different predictors. This is shown in Fig. 3.5a,

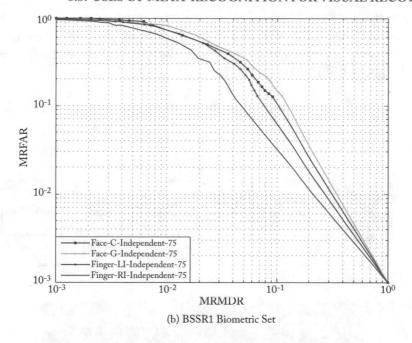

(b) BSSR1 Biometric Set

Figure 3.5: *(Continued.)* MRET curves for the EBGM face recognition algorithm (Okada et al. [1998]) on the FERET dataset (Scheirer et al. [2011]) and BSSR1 (National Institute of Standards and Technology [2004]), NIST's multibiometric data set incorporating scores from two face recognition algorithms and one fingerprint recognition algorithm operating over two different fingers. (b) shows meta-recognition predictions for each modality independently (i.e., the different modalities are not fused together in this experiment). The tail size used in each experiment is noted in the plots. Based on Scheirer et al. [2011].

where basic score thresholding and a T-norm-based score thresholding (Scheirer et al. [2011]) are plotted against a meta-recogntion predictor, which achieves the best performance for that experiment.

3.3   USES OF META-RECOGNITION FOR VISUAL RECOGNITION

Meta-recognition, as we saw above, was first applied to identification problems within the area of biometrics (Scheirer et al. [2011, 2012b]). Subsequent work has applied it to the problem of image correspondence (Fragoso and Turk [2013]), where the ability to triage candidate results through failure prediction can be quite valuable for improving the quality of the final results of a vision system. Along with a new application, the feasibility of an EVT distribution other than the Weibull for meta-recognition has been demonstrated.

Fragoso and Turk [2013] showed that a formulation of meta-recognition that uses the Rayleigh distribution (see Sec. 2.3.5) is effective at improving the performance of guided sampling for feature point matching between images (Fig. 3.6). The Rayleigh distribution's Complementary Cumulative Distribution Function (CCDF) is:

$$R(s, \lambda) = e^{-\frac{s^2}{2\lambda^2}}. \tag{3.4}$$

(a)

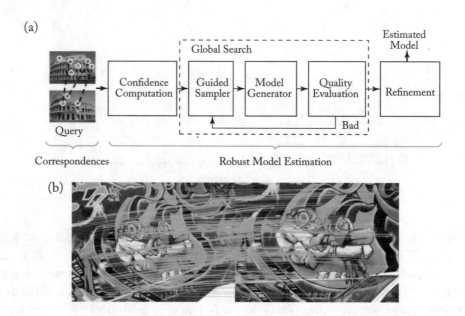

Figure 3.6: Meta-recognition applied to guided sampling for accurate model estimation from image feature correspondences. Panel A: candidate correspondences are evaluated by a meta-recognition algorithm leveraging a Rayleigh model of extrema drawn from the sampling process. A correctness-confidence is computed for each correspondence, with the overall recognition system taking corrective action when poor quality correspondences are identified. Panel B: by incorporating meta-recognition into the feature correspondence problem, Fragoso and Turk showed that better guided sampling can be achieved. Based on Fragoso et al. [2013].

Only a single parameter, the scale λ, must be estimated. This is accomplished by applying the maximum likelihood formula over the top n scores in the tail, skipping the hypothesized outlier:

$$\hat{\lambda} = \sqrt{\frac{1}{2(n-1)} \sum_{i=2}^{n} s_i^2}, \tag{3.5}$$

where s_i is the i-th ranked matching score. Compared with the Weibull parameter estimation, $\hat{\lambda}$ can be computed very efficiently, supporting real-time vision applications.

Meta-recognition with the Rayleigh distribution finds a CCDF that puts most of its mass over the support of the matching score distribution. This support should be mostly to the left of the non-matching score distribution (assuming a scenario where smaller scores are better). Fragoso and Turk argue that there is a distinct advantage to this model: it assigns higher confidence to matching scores that fall to the left of the non-matching score distribution, and much lower confidence to those that fall within it. In contrast, a Weibull will have an abrupt transition at the the crossover point between the distributions. The meta-recognition algorithm in this case is functionally equivalent to Alg. 3.1, but with the Rayleigh distribution taking the place of the Reverse Weibull or Weibull in step 3.

CHAPTER 4

Recognition Score Normalization

In visual recognition, information comes at us from many different sources. Some of these sources may be consistent (e.g., multiple cameras from the same type of sensor), while others may not be (e.g., a collection of different classifiers, trained over different feature spaces). How we combine heterogeneous information has a major impact on the final decision for our recognition task. Remarkably, often little to no consideration is given to this critically important step in the recognition process. For example, imagine two different classifiers that have produced their own individual scores from the same input: 1000.14 for the first classifier, and 2.87 for the second. If we add these two scores without any additional processing, the second classifier will have relatively little impact on the final decision—the sum of 1003.01 isn't very far from the first classifier's original score. Now assume that a probabilistic transformation function (putting both scores between 0.0 and 1.0) has caused the first classifier to end up with a score of 0.15, and the second a score of 0.78. After the application of this *score normalization*, where both scores are put on a consistent basis before they are combined, it's clear that the second classifier actually has *more* impact than the first. Situations like this happen rather frequently, thus normalization is a key element for achieving good classification performance. In this chapter, we will look at probabilistic normalization based on EVT. This methodology is important, as it will provide the basis for the calibrated supervised learning models that will be described in Chapter 5.

4.1 GOALS OF GOOD RECOGNITION SCORE NORMALIZATION

What are the properties that a recognition score normalization algorithm should possess? Consider the following list, which lays out goals from an operational perspective.

- Recognition accuracy should be improved, beyond what a single source of information can achieve.

- The algorithm should be robust in a statistical sense, i.e., the algorithm should not be strongly impacted by outliers.

- Related to the above goal, there should be some measure of fault tolerance if the source of the input is failing.

- Simple parameter estimation should be utilized, with the algorithm not reliant on a large training set for modeling the match and non-match distributions.

- The final output should be probabilistic in nature, leading to a straightforward interpretation of the normalized scores.

We can achieve a number of these goals with basic approaches, including some that make use of central tendency modeling (Jain et al. [2005]). For the following approaches, assume that we have a set of distance or similarity scores $\{s_k\}, k = 1, 2, \ldots, n$.

The most basic strategy that can be deployed is *min-max* normalization. Only two parameters are needed by this normalization model: the minimum score and the maximum score from the set of scores $\{s_k\}$. A normalized min-max score s'_k is calculated via:

$$s'_k = \frac{s_k - \min}{\max - \min}.$$

(4.1)

Unfortunately, this algorithm is strongly impacted by outliers; recalling our discussion of tail modeling from earlier chapters, we have an expectation that the minimum or maximum scores are likely extrema with respect to the overall distribution of scores. There is no guarantee that the minimum or maximum won't be wildly different than the mean or median of $\{s_k\}$, thus providing a very weak normalization.

A better, and more common strategy based on central tendency modeling is $z - score$ normalization. Like min-max, it also relies on just two parameters. But instead of directly applying specific scores as parameters, it uses the mean μ and standard deviation σ statistics calculated over a range of scores at hand, or a set of reference scores from the same recognition algorithm. A normalized z-score s'_k is calculated via:

$$s'_k = \frac{s_k - \mu}{\sigma}.$$

(4.2)

Note that z-score normalization makes a strong assumption that the scores in $\{s_k\}$ are Gaussian distributed. For many problems in visual recognition, this is not the case. Thus there is no expectation of optimality for non-Gaussian score data. Moreover, the mean and standard deviation are strongly impacted by outliers, meaning that like min-max normalization, this technique isn't robust. And z-scores themselves do not fall within a bounded range. Interpreting the scores following normalization can be difficult, and fusion across z-scores calculated from different underlying score distributions may be combining inconsistent data—exactly the situation we were trying to avoid by normalizing in the first place.

Addressing robustness, *median* normalization is far more tolerant to the impact of extrema by virtue of the choice of the statistics used to approximate the parameters of the underlying score distribution. The form of the normalization is similar to the z-score, except that the median is subtracted from each score, and that difference is divided by the Median Absolute Deviation

(MAD) statistic:

$$s'_k = \frac{s_k - \text{median}}{\text{MAD}},$$ (4.3)

where $\text{MAD} = \text{median}(|s_k - \text{median}|)$. Like the z-score, median normalization relies on central tendency modeling. If the underlying score distribution is not Gaussian, this approach is not optimal. Also, its scores are not confined to a fixed range, leading to the same fusion problem described at the beginning of this chapter.

Addressing the deficiencies of the above methods, *tanh-estimators* as a normalization approach bring to bear more sophisticated statistical modeling in the form of Hampel estimators (Hampel et al. [2011]). A normalized score in this case is calculated via:

$$s'_k = \frac{1}{2}\left\{\tanh\left(0.01\left(\frac{s_k - \mu_{GH}}{\sigma_{GH}}\right)\right) + 1\right\}.$$ (4.4)

In the above formulation, the Hampel estimators yield the mean (μ_{GH}) and standard deviation (σ_{GH}) estimates for a given score distribution. The following influence function defines the Hampel estimators:

$$\psi(u) = \begin{cases} u & 0 \le |u| < a, \\ a\,\text{sign}(u) & a \le |u| < b, \\ a\,\text{sign}(u)\left(\frac{c-|u|}{c-b}\right) & b \le |u| < c, \\ 0 & |u| \ge c. \end{cases}$$ (4.5)

In order to be robust, tanh-estimators reduce the influence of the tail in the normalization process. However, to achieve this, the tail points for three different intervals (a, b, c) from the median score of the distribution must be defined in an *ad hoc* manner. These parameters can be difficult to determine experimentally, and if chosen incorrectly, limit the effectiveness of the normalization. Thus we can say that tanh-estimators are robust to noise, but not parameter estimation.

Reconsidering the list at the beginning of this section, it immediately becomes evident that we are not satisfying all of our goals for a good normalization scheme with the most common methods. Most importantly, we are not receiving a reliable probability score as output, nor do we have an expectation that the normalization process itself is robust in a statistical sense. This latter point is worth emphasizing. The varying nature of the underlying distributions of scores across different recognition algorithms often leads to inconsistency in normalization results. Recalling the discussion above, if a normalization technique like the z-score assumes that the algorithms considered for fusion produce scores that follow a Gaussian distribution, and at least one of those distributions is not Gaussian, the results will not be optimal. The distribution of recognition scores is the result of a complex interaction between the algorithm and the data being processed, and it is dangerous to assume too much about it.

Complications are introduced when one or more sensors or recognition algorithms being considered for fusion fail (or, in the case of human biometrics, are intentionally deceived). We know from Chapter 3 that failure in a recognition system occurs when an input sample of one class is recognized as being a member of another class, or when an input sample that should be recognized by the system is rejected as being unknown. The scores produced in these failure scenarios become problematic for normalization techniques, especially when they resemble an "expected" (and often estimated) match distribution. What we need is a probabilistic normalization scheme that is not only robust, but tolerant in the face of possibly drastic failure. To achieve this, let's consider a normalization formulation based on EVT (Fig. 4.1).

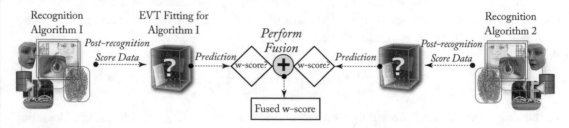

Figure 4.1: An overview of the w-score normalization process for two different visual recognition algorithms. Recognition scores are produced by the algorithms for the given input. An EVT model (Weibull) is fit to the tail of the sorted scores from each algorithm. The normalization of these score sequences is performed using the CDF of the resulting Weibull distributions (hence w-scores). The w-score is an estimate of the probability of a particular score not being from the non-match distribution, and hence a good normalization for score-level fusion. Using a simple fusion strategy like the sum rule, w-scores can be combined and checked against a threshold to make a final decision. From Scheirer et al. [2010].

4.2   W-SCORE NORMALIZATION

Before delving into the specifics of an algorithm for EVT-based normalization, let's recall what we learned about the operation of the meta-recognition algorithm from Chapter 3. When we fit a Weibull or Reverse Weibull distribution to a set of scores hypothesized to be from the non-match distribution, we created a model that would help us predict if incoming scores were outliers with respect to that distribution. This was done in order to determine if a given score is indicative of a successful match (i.e., is an outlier with respect to the non-match distribution), or a failed match (i.e., is not an outlier with respect to the non-match distribution). How can we use the same statistical fitting procedure for normalization? Given a raw score and an EVT model, the score's normalization becomes the formal probability of it being an outlier in the extreme value "non-match" model, and hence its chance of being a successful recognition instance. Like meta-recognition, the procedure only requires the scores from a single recognition instance for a particular recognition algorithm—no training data or elaborate hand-tuning is necessary. With this, we have a normalization model that is inherently tolerant to failure.

Algorithm 4.2 w-score normalization technique

Require: A collection of scores $\{s_k\}$, of vector length m, from a single recognition algorithm j;

1: **Sort** and retain the n best (largest or smallest) scores, $s_1, \ldots, s_n \in \{s_k\}$;
2: **Fit** a Reverse Weibull or Weibull distribution W to $s_2, \ldots, s_n$, skipping the hypothesized outlier;
3: **while** $k < m$ **do**
4:     $s'_k = \text{CDF}(s_k, W)$
5:     $k \leftarrow k + 1$
6: **end while**

Keeping this general idea in mind, let's look at the description of the Weibull-score (or w-score for short) procedure in Alg. 4.2. The precondition for the normalization is a collection of scores $\{s_k\}$ from a single recognition algorithm. These scores are then sorted (line 1), and, as was done for the meta-recognition algorithm, a Reverse Weibull (if the scores are bounded from above) or Weibull distribution (if the scores are bounded from below) is fit to the scores (line 2). As w-scores are based on the fitting of the Weibull model to the non-match data of the top scores, an issue that must be addressed is the impact of any outliers on the fitting. For rank-1 fitting, where the top score is the expected match data, this bias is easily reduced by excluding the top score and fitting to the remaining $n - 1$ scores from the top n. If the top score is an outlier (recognition is correct), then excluding it does not impact the fitting. If the top score was not a match, including this recognition in the fitting will bias the distribution to be broader than it should, which will produce lower probability scores for the correct match and most of the non-matches.

In addition, we must address the choice of n, the tail size to be used in fitting. This tail size represents the only parameter that must be estimated for w-scores. Including too few scores might reduce accuracy, including too many items could impact assumptions of portfolio sampling. However, in studies making use of the w-score (Scheirer et al. [2010]), even very small tail sizes (3 and 5) produce good normalization results. That is consistent with work in other fields (Kotz and Nadarajah [2001]), where 3-5 is a very common fitting size range for the Weibull distribution. For more discussion on the selection of tail size, see Sec. 2.4.

Once the fitting has taken place, we have all of the information necessary to complete the normalization. For every gallery class i, let score $s'_{i,j}$ be its normalized score in the collection of scores $\{s_k\}$ for algorithm j. The CDF defined by the parameters of the fitting W is used to produce the normalized probability score $s'_{i,j}$ (line 4). To fuse w-scores, the sum rule can be applied:

$$f_i = \sum_j s'_{i,j}. \tag{4.6}$$

Alternatively, similar to Eq. 4.6, one can consider the sum of only those items with a w-score (probability of success) above some given threshold, or could consider products or likelihood ratios of the w-scores.

Now that the w-score algorithm has been introduced, let's step through the process in code using libMR. The following example normalizes two different score sequences drawn from different score distributions. Assume that the arrays `tail1[]` and `tail2[]` hold the distance scores from the lower tails of two sets of scores drawn from two different recognition algorithms. Note that both sets of scores appear to be in different ranges. The procedures we will invoke to do the normalization are very similar to the ones we discussed in Chapter 3 for meta-recognition.

Instead of using just one MetaRecognition object, we will need to instantiate two to accommodate fittings for both tails. Thus, the MetaRecognition objects `mr1` and `mr2` are instantiated with the option "true," meaning the hypothesized outlier (i.e., the lowest score) is skipped during fitting. Next, a Weibull distribution is fit to the nine scores from both tails via the `FitLow()` function; parameters for the individual normalization models are stored within the `mr1` and `mr2` objects. As with the meta-recognition models, `Save()` can be called to preserve the models on disk so that they can be used in the future without recomputing the fitting.

```c
#include <stdio.h>
#include "libMR/MetaRecognition.h"

int main(int argc, char **argv)
{
  double tail1[] = {0.25419999999999998, 0.32952, 0.34912, 0.35493,
  0.35500, 0.35598, 0.35705, 0.35721, 0.35756, 0.35921};

  double tail2[] = {1.81110, 1.85104, 1.85288, 1.85312,
  1.85566, 1.855691, 1.856991, 1.856999, 1.857124, 1.85771};

  double wscore;
  int length = sizeof(tail1) / sizeof(double);

  MetaRecognition mr1(true);
  mr1.FitLow(tail1, length);
  mr1.Save((char*) "mr1.txt");

  MetaRecognition mr2(true);
  mr2.FitLow(tail2, length);
  mr2.Save((char*) "mr2.txt");

  for (int i = 0; i < 4; i++)
  {
   if (i == 0)
     printf("w-scores for tail 1, fitting on tail 1: ");
```

```
     else if (i == 1)
      printf("w-scores for tail 1, fitting on tail 2: ");
     else if (i == 2)
      printf("w-scores for tail 2, fitting on tail 2: ");
     else
      printf("w-scores for tail 2, fitting on tail 1: ");
     for (int j = 0; j < length; j++)
     {
      if (i == 0)
      {
       wscore = mr1.CDF(tail1[j]);
      }
      else if (i == 1)
      {
       wscore = mr2.CDF(tail1[j]);
      }
      else if (i == 2)
      {
       wscore = mr2.CDF(tail2[j]);
      }
      else
      {
       wscore = mr1.CDF(tail2[j]);
      }
      printf("%d:%f ", j, wscore);
     }
     printf("\n\n");
    }
}
```

A major difference between the above code and the code we looked at in Chapter 3 is the way we use the Weibull models following fitting. Instead of calling Predict_Match() to make a meta-recognition prediction, we call the CDF() function to normalize a raw distance score into a probability value. In this example, we calculate normalized scores in four different configurations: (1) normalizing the scores in tail1[] using the parameters in mr1 for the model we fit to that tail; (2) normalizing the scores in tail1[] using the parameters in mr2 for the model we fit to tail2[]; (3) normalizing the scores in tail2[] using the parameters in mr2 for the model we fit to that tail; and (4) normalizing the scores in tail2[] using the parameters in mr1 for the model we fit to tail1[].

To compile this code, first copy the above self-contained program to the library directory libMR/examples as wscore-test.cpp. Then run make from the libMR/build/examples directory. After wscore-test is executed, the following output should be observed:

```
$ ./wscore-test
w-scores for tail 1, fitting on tail 1: 0:1.000000 1:0.992121
2:0.589931 3:0.417102 4:0.415203 5:0.389182 6:0.362019 7:0.358073
8:0.349544 9:0.311312

w-scores for tail 1, fitting on tail 2: 0:1.000000 1:1.000000
2:1.000000 3:1.000000 4:1.000000 5:1.000000 6:1.000000 7:1.000000
8:1.000000 9:1.000000

w-scores for tail 2, fitting on tail 2: 0:1.000000 1:0.976806
2:0.814992 3:0.781224 4:0.394735 5:0.390641 6:0.244988 7:0.244249
8:0.232939 9:0.185674

w-scores for tail 2, fitting on tail 1: 0:0.000000 1:0.000000
2:0.000000 3:0.000000 4:0.000000 5:0.000000 6:0.000000 7:0.000000
8:0.000000 9:0.000000
```

Let's try to understand what happened during the normalization process that yielded different w-scores in each of the four normalization instances. In the first case, the model comes from the same set of scores being normalized, thus the results are what we expect: the lowest raw scores map to the highest probabilities (recall that for these distance scores, lower is better). In stark contrast, something very different has happened in the second case, where the model comes from the second set of scores, but the scores we are normalizing haven't changed: all of the scores were normalized to 1.0. Glancing at the raw scores in the code snippet, the scores in tail1[] are an order of magnitude smaller than those in tail2[], from which the model applied in this case was derived. Recall that we are using the *cumulative* distribution function of the model to generate the w-scores. Because the scores in tail1[] fall to the left of the lowest score in tail2[], they must receive a value of 1.0. We observe the opposite effect in the fourth case, where the scores in tail2[] are far to the right of those in tail1[], making them improbable (0.0) under the parameters of the model for the first tail.

The w-score fusion possesses a unique robust property, providing built-in error detection. Generating scores from the CDF allows us to estimate the "confidence" of particular measurement (refer to the discussion of the hypothesis test in Sec. 3.2.3). Considering the probabilities for the top score for each algorithm, we can determine if it is highly likely that the final fused score f_1 is not a non-match; if a particular algorithm consistently fails, we have evidence of a possible error, most probably some type of data misalignment. Algorithm 4.3 describes the process of the error

---

Algorithm 4.3 w-score error detection for fusion

Require: A collection of w-scores S'_n, where n is the number of algorithms to fuse, and the collection has m different score vectors for each algorithm;

Require: Algorithm FRR/FAR at current settings or ground-truth for each recognition instance;

Require: A significance threshold ϵ and an error percentage threshold $\mathcal{T}$;

1: **while** $i < m$ **do**
2:   **while** $j < n$ **do**
3:     $f_1 \leftarrow f_1 + s'_{i,j,1}$
4:   **end while**
5:   **if** not a match **then**
6:     **if** $f_1 \geq n \times \epsilon$ **then**
7:       PossibleMatches $\leftarrow$ PossibleMatches $+1$
8:     **end if**
9:   **end if**
10:   $i \leftarrow i + 1$
11: **end while**
12: **if** PossibleMatches $\geq m \times \mathcal{T}$ **then**
13:   **return** System Error Detected
14: **end if**

---

detection. A count of the possible matches is kept, and if it exceeds $\mathcal{T}$ percent, we declare a system error. This error detection property is useful for indicating three possible errors.

1. The Reverse Weibull or Weibull fitting is inaccurate for valid score data (due to a mis-estimated tail size).

2. Invalid score data (from parsing errors) produced a CDF that returns an improbably large number of high w-scores.

3. An error is present in alignment or the ground-truth labeling (off-by-one errors due to bad pre-processing).

4.3   EMPIRICAL EVALUATION OF W-SCORE FUSION

What kind of results can be achieved with the w-score approach in practice? Let's consider two different popular applications of visual recognition in computer vision. In multi-biometric fusion, the objective is to achieve higher accuracy in determining the identity of a subject by considering multiple sources of biometric information (e.g., the face and fingerprints of a subject). This could be in a 1:1 verification mode, where there is a claimed identity for authentication purposes, or a 1:N identification mode, where an unknown subject is matched against a database of known subjects. Here we will consider the latter case of biometric identification, as it is inherently suitable for the w-score algorithm by virtue of always providing a sequence of scores. In content-based image retrieval (CBIR), the objective is to find all of the images in a database that are similar in content to a query image. This is another example of a problem that produces sequences of scores (usually distance-based) as part of its operation, and is thus also suitable for w-score normalization when the scores from a variety of different descriptor comparisons are to be fused to improve accuracy. The fusion process is the same in both cases: normalization followed by the application of the sum rule (Eq. 4.6).

To understand if the w-score is helpful for fusion, let's compare it to the z-score, which we introduced in Sec. 4.1 as a commonly deployed normalization strategy. A convenient way to represent any change in performance is percentage reduction in error (i.e., improvement). Assume that for recognition, we are interested in the rank-1 result (i.e., the top result out of a ranked list of results). Let $\%e_z$ be the percentage of incorrect rank-1 results for z-score fusion, and $\%e_w$ be the percentage of incorrect rank-1 results for w-score fusion. Percentage reduction in error is then calculated as:

$$\%reduction = (\%e_z - \%e_w)/\%e_z. \tag{4.7}$$

A summary plot expressing the results for four sets of experiments from Scheirer et al. [2010] can be found in Fig. 4.2.

The first set of experiments tests a series of biometric recognition algorithms from the NIST BSSR1 (National Institute of Standards and Technology [2004]) biometric score set. The data set consists of scores from two face recognition algorithms and one fingerprint recognition algorithm applied to two different fingers. BSSR1's multibiometric subset contains 517 score sets for each of the algorithms, with common subjects between each set. BSSR1 also contains individual score subsets for all algorithms, where the scores do not have common subjects between them. Out of this individual score set data, a "chimera" data set was created. Chimera data sets in biometrics are composed of individual modalities from different subjects (e.g., the face from one person and an index finger from a different person to form a single artificial identity), and are used in algorithm evaluation to address limitations in available data sets. For BSSR1 in its default mode, fusion pushes the recognition rate close to 100% for even weak normalizations. The chimera data set considered here contains 3,000 score sets and consistent labeling across all algorithms. It is signifantly more difficult than the BSSR1 multibiometric subset. Different experiments were run for different combinations of the face recognition algorithms and results for different fingers.

As has been emphasized throughout this book, the choice of tail size matters for the performance one can expect from any EVT-based method. Note that in exhaustive experimentation, better performance than z-scores was always achieved when choosing the correct tail size for fitting, and fusing scores within the tail used for fitting. The tail size used for fitting for this set of experiments was 5. Glancing at Fig. 4.2, there is an advantage for using w-scores over z-scores with this particular parameter setting for both the original and chimera BSSR1 data sets.

More interesting though is an analysis of performance when recognition algorithm failure is present. The second set of experiments tests fusion behavior in a failure scenario, where rank-1

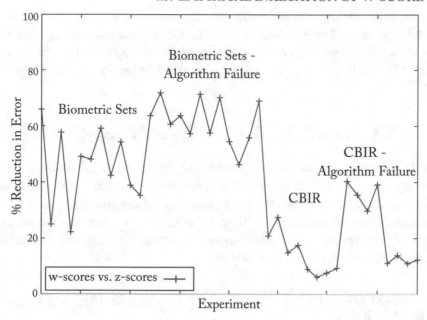

Figure 4.2: When applied across different visual recognition problems, w-score fusion demonstrates a good measure of improvement over more conventional normalizations like z-scores — especially in cases where at least one algorithm providing information for the fusion process is failing. This plot summarizes a series of experiments for multi-biometric fusion (National Institute of Standards and Technology [2004]) and content-based image retrieval (Datta et al. [2008], Jégou et al. [2008], Stehling et al. [2002]). Results are expressed as percentage reduction in error (i.e., improvement) compared to z-scores. Based on Scheirer et al. [2010].

recognition for at least one of the algorithms is 0%. For biometrics, this may be thought of as an "impostor" test, where a subject is trying to actively defeat the recognition system. For example, consider the possibility of a facial disguise that causes a face algorithm to fail, but has no effect on a fingerprint recognition algorithm. Turning again to the results in Fig. 4.2, w-scores have a strong advantage over z-scores for regular fusion, and a significant advantage in cases where a recognition algorithm is failing.

Turning to w-score normalization for CBIR, a series of simple CBIR descriptors (Datta et al. [2008]) can also be considered for fusion. The last two sets of experiments make use of data from the Corel "Relevants" set (Stehling et al. [2002]), containing 50 unique classes, and the INRIA "Holidays" set (Jégou et al. [2008]), containing 500 unique classes. Using a variety of descriptors, 1,624 score sets were generated for Corel Relevants and 1,491 score sets were generated for INRIA Holidays. In total, 47 different combinations of descriptors were tested across all experiments in Scheirer et al. [2010]; 4 representative combinations from this set are shown in

Fig. 4.2. The experiments are identical to those of the biometric sets described above, including the basic fusion test and failure test. Similar to the multibiometric fusion case, in all of the fusion experiments with CBIR descriptors, w-scores outperformed z-scores when the appropriate tail size was chosen for Weibull fitting. The tail sized used for fitting for all CBIR experiments was 3.

4.4   OTHER INSTANTIATIONS OF EVT NORMALIZATION

The Weibull-based normalization is just one approach for EVT normalization. Other work has surfaced recently exploring different distributions around the same basic normalization paradigm that has been introduced in this chapter. This section highlights some of the more interesting research directions. Note that while some of these techniques have a distinct meta-recognition flavor, all specifically incorporate score normalization into their operation, which meta-recognition as described in Chapter 3 does not inherently do.

4.4.1   GEV-BASED NORMALIZATION: EXTREME VALUE SAMPLE CONSENSUS

Score candidates for normalization appear across many algorithms in computer vision, and not just as the outputs of classifiers for object recognition or biometrics. Image correspondence is a classic problem in the field, which underpins the estimation of model parameters such as homographies and fundamental matrices. In Sec. 3.3, we looked at the application of meta-recognition to image correspondence scores. Given that the distance between a query and reference image is the primary mode of similarity assessment, the process is amenable to score-based normalization for determining the suitability of the match hypothesis. It is well known that correspondences are often highly impacted by outliers, which resemble true correspondences, but are really artifacts induced by sensor noise or an imprecise feature model. The conventional approach to this problem is an application of Random Sample Consensus (RANSAC) (Fischler and Bolles [1981]), or one of its many variants (Chum et al. [2003], Raguram and Frahm [2011], Raguram et al. [2008], Sattler et al. [2009], Torr and Zisserman [2000]), which mitigates the impact of outliers. However, if the percentage of inliers is low (e.g., $< 10\%$), the triage process for selecting correct matching hypotheses is slowed down considerably.

To address this, Fragoso et al. [2013] introduced an EVT-based method that assigns a confidence value to each match in order to accelerate hypothesis generation. The algorithm is dubbed Extreme Value Sample Consensus (EVSAC). It is, in essence, a nearest neighbor matching algorithm that relies on score normalization to assess distance in a probabilistic space. In a nutshell, the algorithm makes use of two distributional fittings to assign a final confidence score to a matching instance. The first is an application of the Gamma distribution (National Institute of Standards and Technology [2012]) to model the distribution of matching scores F_c. The second is an application of the GEV distribution, which we discussed in Sec. 2.3.4, to model $G_{\bar{c}}$, the distribution of minimums from the distribution of non-matching scores $F_{\bar{c}}$. An overview of the process is shown in Fig. 4.3.

Walking through the algorithm in detail, let's first assume that the confidence value of the nearest neighbor score $s_{i,j*}$ is modeled by a mixture distribution:

$$F = \varepsilon F_c + (1 - \varepsilon)G_{\bar{c}}, \tag{4.8}$$

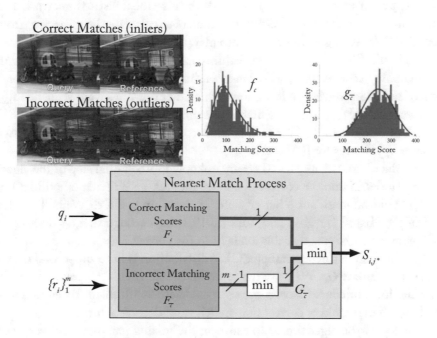

Figure 4.3: An overview of the matching model underpinning the EVSAC method introduced by Fragoso et al. [2013]. RANSAC-based algorithms can be slow when the percentage of correct correspondences is small. EVSAC assigns confidence values to each matching correspondence, thus accelerating the generation of hypothesis models for RANSAC. (Top) From a matching instance between a query image and reference image, the matching scores can be separated into correct matches (f_c) and incorrect matches ($g_{\bar{c}}$). The PDFs of these score distributions are shown in the figure. (Bottom) EVSAC is a probabilistic EVT-based framework for matching a query descriptor $\mathbf{q}_i$ to a set of reference descriptors $\{\mathbf{r}_j\}_{j=1}^{m}$. Assume that a random process generates at most one correct matching score using the CDF F_c. Also assume that a different random process generates at least $m - 1$ incorrect matching scores using the CDF $F_{\bar{c}}$. The minimum is taken from this set of incorrect matches, modeled by the CDF $G_{\bar{c}}$. The nearest match process then takes the minimum of the scores coming from $F_{\bar{c}}$ and $G_{\bar{c}}$, which is the best matching score $s_{i,j*}$. The objective of the EVSAC algorithm is to compute the confidence that $s_{i,j*}$ is a correct match, without prior knowledge of the distributions. From Fragoso et al. [2013].

where the inlier ratio ε is the mixing parameter between the distribution of matching scores F_c and the distribution of minimums $G_{\bar{c}}$ from the distribution of non-matching scores. This mixture model is used to calculate weights (i.e., confidences) as a function of a matching score for every correspondence by computing the posterior probability using Eq. 4.8:

$$p(c|s) = \frac{p(s|c)p(c)}{p(s|c)p(c) + p(s|\bar{c})p(\bar{c})} = \frac{\varepsilon f_c}{\varepsilon f_c + (1 - \varepsilon)g_{\bar{c}}}, \tag{4.9}$$

where $p(c) = \varepsilon$, $p(s|c) = f_c$, and $p(s|\bar{c}) = g_{\bar{c}}$. With this probabilistic framework, the question then becomes how to estimate the necessary parameters to calculate the posteriors from Eq. 4.9. This is where the EVSAC algorithm comes into play.

As input, EVSAC requires the image feature correspondences $\{\mathbf{x} \leftrightarrow \mathbf{x}'\}_{i=1}^n$ and the k nearest neighbor matching scores $\{s_{i,1:k}\}$ sorted in ascending order for every i-th correspondence. For the purposes of notation in what follows, the r-th element of the sorted sequence $s_{i,1:k}$ for the i-th match is denoted as $s_{i,(r)}$. Thus, the first nearest matching score is $s_{i,(1)} = s_{i,j*}$. EVSAC will calculate the set of weights $\{w\}_{i=1}^n$ for each of the n correspondences. These weights will then be used to generate hypotheses for RANSAC.

Note that the distributions F_c and $G_{\bar{c}}$ are unknown—the initial step of the algorithm is to estimate them. To determine the correct match candidates, an *ad hoc* method like Lowe's ratio (Lowe [2004]) could be used, but a better tactic is something akin to Weibull- (Scheirer et al. [2011]) or Rayleigh-based (Fragoso and Turk [2013]) meta-recognition, as discussed in Chapter 3. A two-parameter Gamma distribution is fit to the correct match candidates, providing the estimate of F_c. Similarly, a three-parameter GEV distribution is fit to the second nearest matching scores $s_{i,(2)}$ to estimate $G_{\bar{c}}$. Why use the second nearest matching scores and not defer to the predictor? Predictions, of course, have some error associated with them. By choosing the second nearest matches, a better yield of correct non-match candidates is achieved.

The next step of the algorithm is to estimate the mixing parameter between the two distributions ε. That process begins by computing the empirical CDF of the mixture distribution F from Eq. 4.8 using all of the lowest matching scores $s_{i,(1)}$. ε can then be estimated by solving the following constrained least-squares problem:

$$\min_{\mathbf{y}} \frac{1}{2}||A\mathbf{y} - \mathbf{b}||_2^2 \text{ subject to } \mathbf{1}^\mathsf{T}\mathbf{y} = 1, 0 \preceq \mathbf{y} \preceq \mathbf{u}, \tag{4.10}$$

where the $\preceq$ symbol indicates entry-wise comparison, and

$$A = \begin{bmatrix} F_c(s_1) & G_{\bar{c}}(s_1) \\ \vdots & \vdots \\ F_c(s_L) & G_{\bar{c}}(s_L) \end{bmatrix}, \quad \mathbf{b} = \begin{bmatrix} F(s_1) \\ \vdots \\ F(s_L) \end{bmatrix}, \quad \mathbf{y} = \begin{bmatrix} \varepsilon \\ \varepsilon' \end{bmatrix}, \quad \text{and } \mathbf{u} = \begin{bmatrix} \zeta \\ 1 \end{bmatrix}.$$

In the above formulation, ζ is the inlier ratio computed by the chosen predictor in the initial step of finding correct match candidates. This is an upper bound: as noted above, the prediction process can be error-prone, thus the true inlier ration must be less than or equal to ζ.

Algorithm 4.4 EVSAC

Require: $\{\mathbf{x} \leftrightarrow \mathbf{x}'\}_{i=1}^{n}$ and $\{s_{i,1:k}\}$;
Ensure: $\{w_i\}_{i=1}^{n}$ and $\{p_i\}_{i=1}^{n}$
  1: $\mathbf{v} \leftarrow \text{Predict}\left(\{s_{i,1:k}\}_{i=1}^{n}\right)$
  2: $(\alpha, \beta) \leftarrow \text{FitGamma}\left(\{s_{i,(1)} \text{ such that } v_i = 1\}\right)$
  3: $(\kappa, \lambda, \tau) \leftarrow \text{FitGEV}\left(\{s_{i,(2)}\}\right)$
  4: Calculate the empirical CDF using $s_{i,j*}$
  5: Find ε by solving Eq. 4.10
  6: Calculate posterior-weights p_i using Eq. 4.9
  7: Calculate weights w_i using Eq. 4.11
  8: Use the weights w_i for generating hypotheses

With ε in hand, the correctness confidence for each correspondence can be calculated by solving Eq. 4.9. This confidence scores is not the final weight, however. Fragoso and Turk warn that overlap between distributions can lead to incorrect matches being assigned a high confidence score. In the context of RANSAC, this means that the algorithm may run slower and not faster as intended. This can be fixed by checking for agreement between the initial correct match predictor and the posterior from Eq. 4.9. In line with this, the final weights are calculated as:

$$w_i = p_i v_i, \tag{4.11}$$

where p_i is the posterior and v_i is the prediction for the i-th match. The complete EVSAC algorithm, summarizing all of these steps, is shown below in Alg. 4.4.

Using the same general normalization principles we laid out earlier in this chapter, EVSAC achieves impressive results for homography and fundamental matrix estimation. In experiments over Balanced Exploration and Exploitation Model Search (BEEM) (Goshen and Shimshoni [2008]), Balanced Local and Global Search (BLOGS) (Brahmachari and Sarkar [2009]), Progressive Sample Consensus (PROSAC) (Chum and Matas [2005]), and Guided Maximum Likelihood Estimation Sample Consensus (GMLESAC) (Tordoff and Murray [2002]), Fragoso et al. [2013] showed that EVSAC is more accurate and faster when the inlier ratio is low ($< 11\%$). Low inlier rations are typically associated with complex scenes, which are challenges for many visual recognition algorithms. As the inlier ratio increases ($> 20\%$) EVSAC remains comparable to the non-EVT methods.

4.4.2 GEV-BASED NORMALIZATION: GEV-KMEANS

Another important problem in visual recognition is unsupervised data clustering, which is not constrained by the need for large labeled training data sets like supervised classification (which we will look at in the next chapter). Further, it can help us learn relevant features, which is an attractive data-driven paradigm that in principle should lead to better results when compared to domain-agnostic handcrafted features (e.g., Scale-invariant feature transform (SIFT), Histogram of Oriented Gradients (HOG), Local Binary Patterns (LBP). The most common clustering approach is the K-means algorithm (Lloyd [1982]). It partitions n observations into K different clusters, where each observation is grouped with the cluster with the closest mean value. Li et al. [2012] describe an improved K-means clustering algorithm meant to better tolerate outliers, based on the GEV distribution. GEV-Kmeans normalizes the Minimal Squared Distances (MSD) from a point to all K cluster centers based on a GEV model. EVT applies in this case because with a large enough K, MSD empirically conforms to the GEV distribution.

To begin, first consider the objective function for the K-means clustering algorithm. Given a set of observations $(x_1, x_2, \ldots, x_N)$, where $x_i \in \mathbb{R}^d$, K-means attempts to partition the N observations into K sets $C = \{C_1, C_2, \ldots, C_K\}$. This can be expressed as the following minimization problem:

$$\min_{\{c_k\}} \quad J = \frac{1}{N} \sum_i \min_k \{\|x_i - c_k\|^2\} \equiv \frac{1}{N} \sum_i y_i, \tag{4.12}$$

where y_i is the MSD of x_i to all centers: $y_i = \min_k \{\|x_i - c_1\|^2, \ldots, \|x_i - c_K\|^2\}$.

Let's try to understand a bit more about why K-means leads to an extreme value problem. As an MSD, y_i must be a block minimum among all K squared distances. Equation 4.12 can be connected to the GEV distribution by defining a random variable $D = \|X - CL\|^2$, where $L \in \mathbb{R}^K$ is a random variable that indicates which cluster X is in by setting one of its dimensions to 1. A new random variable can be defined by sampling L K' times, where K' need not be the same as K:

$$Y = \min_{\text{all } K' \text{samples}} \{\|X - CL_1\|^2, \ldots, \|X - CL_{K'}\|^2\}. \tag{4.13}$$

Each of these squared distances is an i.i.d. sample of the random variable D. The minimization problem yields block minima, which are extrema that must be modeled using an EVT distribution. But why GEV? Li et al. conclude that the Type II form, which is the Fréchet distribution, should be used based on the bounds of the data. However, recall from Chapter 2 that GEV is a generalization of all three extreme value distribution types, and thus must also apply for this very same case (given the bounds, it is possible that the Weibull distribution would apply here as well). Moreover, there is some precedent for using the GEV for visual recognition tasks (see Burghouts et al. [2008], Fernando et al. [2010], Scheirer et al. [2011]).

Also recall from Chapter 2 that the GEV is an extreme value distribution for maxima. Thus, a transformation of the block minima to maxima must take place to invoke it. The optimization of K-means with GEV normalizing the distances y_i is:

$$\min_{\{c_k\}} \quad J = \mathbb{E}_{P(Y)} Y \quad \text{s.t.} : \{\kappa^*, \lambda^*, \tau^*\} = \text{argmax} \sum_{i=1}^{N} \log P(y_i | \kappa, \lambda, \tau), \tag{4.14}$$
$$1 + \kappa^*(y_i - \tau^*)/\lambda^* > 0, \forall i$$

Algorithm 4.5 GEV-Kmeans

1: Initialize $\{c_k\}$;

2: (Optional) Run K-means algorithm several steps;

3: **repeat**

4:      Calculate minimum squared distance y_i;

5:      fit the GEV model using y_i to get (κ, λ, τ);

6:      update centers $\{c_k\}$ using Eq. 4.16;

7: **until** convergence

---

where κ, λ, τ define a GEV distribution fit to the observed training data, and $\mathbb{E}_{P(Y)}$ is the expectation of Y with respect to the distribution of $P(Y)$. In other words, this optimization minimizes MSD with respect to the GEV model.

Li et al. suggest a simplified optimization that constructs Y from the current cluster centers. The resulting optimization problem is:

$$\min_{\kappa, \lambda, \tau, \{c_k\}} \quad J = \alpha \left(\frac{1}{N} \sum_{i=1}^{N} y_i \right) - \frac{1}{N} \sum_{i=1}^{N} \log P(y_i | \kappa, \lambda, \tau), \tag{4.15}$$
$$\text{s.t.} : \ 1 + \kappa(y_i - \tau)/\lambda > 0, \forall i$$

where $\mathbb{E}_{P(Y)}$ has been swapped with empirical expectation, and α is a penalty term. To solve Eq. 4.15, an expectation-maximization-like algorithm can be used. The GEV parameters are estimated by fixing centers (via MLE), and the centers are updated by fixing the GEV parameters. The update rule for the centers is:

$$c_k^* = \sum_{i \in k} \underbrace{\left(\frac{\alpha + A_i + B_i}{\Sigma_{j \in k}(\alpha + A_j + B_j)} \right) x_i}_{w_i} \tag{4.16}$$

$$A_i = \frac{1 + \kappa}{\lambda} \times \frac{1}{1 + \kappa \frac{y_i - \tau}{\lambda}} \qquad B_i = \frac{-1}{\lambda} \left[1 + \kappa \frac{y_i - \tau}{\lambda} \right]^{-1/\kappa - 1},$$

where $i \in k$ means all points have minimal Euclidean distance with respect to the k-th cluster. The complete process is summarized in Alg. 4.5.

How well does this algorithm perform in practice for the task of unsupervised feature learning? Li et al. compared GEV-Kmeans to regular K-means on the CFAR-10 data set (Krizhevsky and Hinton [2009]) for visual object recognition. CFAR-10 contains ten visual object classes and 50K/10K training/testing color images, each of size 32×32. The feature learning process involves mapping local 6×6 patches from the images to a sparse feature vector using the cluster centers. For a range of K values (0–4,000), GEV-Kmeans outperformed K-means when used to extract features for a linear SVM classifier. However, Li et al. note diminishing returns when the value of K is high. At $K = 4,000$, both approaches converge to roughly the same accuracy.

4.4.3   PARETO-BASED NORMALIZATION: IMAGE RETRIEVAL AS OUTLIER DETECTION

Similar to the Weibull- and GEV-based normalization methods we've discussed, Furon and Jégou [2013] describe an outlier detection methodology that normalizes scores coming out of a CBIR system. Recall from the last chapter that the goal of CBIR is to find the set of images that is most similar to a query image. As we saw when examining the w-score process, such an application is ideal for EVT modeling because it provides an ordered list of results by score as an inherent part of its operation. Instead of Weibull or Rayleigh modeling, Furon and Jégou suggest the use of the GPD (see Chapter 2, Sec. 2.3.6). And different from the block maxima / minima modeling we've discussed thus far, Pareto modeling embodies the notion of *peak over threshold*, where extrema are exceedances over a set threshold. We introduced this idea in Chapter 2 as the second extreme value theorem. In image retrieval, a threshold exists to separate relevant and irrelevant matches, making Pareto a reasonable choice of distribution in this case. Outlier detection is meant to eliminate large scores that are attached to incorrect image matches.

The algorithm begins by estimating the GPD parameters. Assume that a sequence of values $x_1, x_2, \ldots, x_n$ is available from a search task, and that the sequence has already been sorted in decreasing order: $x_1 > x_2 > \ldots > x_n$. With respect to the threshold, which we will call u, it is set to a rank that will produce a top-k list for consideration as valid matching results: $u = x_k$. The values above the threshold are established as $y_i = x_i - u$ for $1 \leq i \leq k$. These constraints force $k \ll n$, which means the second extreme value theorem applies, and hence the GPD. Similar to the choice of tail size for the Weibull and GEV fittings we discussed earlier, the choice of rank k affects the quality of the resulting model. Furon and Jégou recommend that k should be some tenths of the data, so that n must be in the thousands. MLE is applied to find the shape (κ) and scale (λ) parameters of the GPD:

$$\ell(\kappa, \lambda) = -k\log\lambda - (1 + 1/\kappa) \sum_{i=1}^{k} \log(1 + \kappa y_i/\lambda). \qquad (4.17)$$

Furon and Jégou make note of some numerical instabilities, which can be dealt with via special estimation cases (see p. 12 of Furon and Jégou [2013]).

The output of the score normalization process should be scores that we can use to detect outliers. For this problem, extrema are treated in a negative sense—the largest scores may be large because they are outliers from the relevant set of images, and extreme values drawn from a vast set of irrelevant images. The approach outlined by Furon and Jégou determines whether or not the largest score x_1 is distributed according to the Generalized Pareto distribution with parameters estimated from the values above the threshold $\{y_i\}_{i=1}^{k}$. This is done by considering x_1 as an empirical quantile of the distribution $F(x)$. Since x_i is the largest score over a set of size n, it should be close to the theoretical quantile $F^{-1}(1 - 1/n)$. However, the probability distribution $F(x)$ that the random variables x are drawn from is unknown. Let $p = 1 - 1/n$. To approximate $F(x)$, we only need its expression around $F^{-1}(p)$, which is greater than u. We'll

---

Algorithm 4.6 Outlier detection for content-based image retrieval

---

1: **while** $d = 1$ **do**
2:    $(\hat{\kappa}, \hat{\underline{\lambda}})$ are estimated from $\mathcal{Y}$ by Eq. 4.17
3:    The detection prediction is made by Eq. 4.19 based on $(\hat{\kappa}, \hat{\underline{\lambda}})$
4:    **if** $d = 1$ **then**
5:        $n_o \leftarrow n_o + 1, \mathcal{Y} \leftarrow \mathcal{Y} \setminus y_{n_o}$
6:    **end if**
7: **end while**
8: **return** $s_i = H(y_k; \hat{\kappa}, \hat{\underline{\lambda}})$ along with n_o

---

call this expression $x^{(p)}$, and it is calculated via:

$$x^{(p)} \approx \begin{cases} u + \hat{\underline{\lambda}}((k/np)^{\hat{\kappa}} - 1)/\hat{\kappa} & \text{if} \quad \hat{\kappa} \neq 0 \\ u + \hat{\underline{\lambda}}\log(k/np) & \text{if} \quad \hat{\kappa} = 0. \end{cases} \quad (4.18)$$

Finally, for a given data point x_1, we can determine if it is an outlier ($d = 1$) or not ($d = 0$) by:

$$d = (\Phi((x_1 - x^{(p)})/\lambda_p) > 1 - \alpha, \quad (4.19)$$

where $\Phi(x)$ is the Gaussian distribution and α is the probability of a false positive.

Putting the above pieces together, a complete algorithm for outlier detection can be formulated (Alg. 4.6). The set of observations above the threshold is denoted as $\mathcal{Y} = \{y_i\}_{i=1}^k$. n_o stores the number of outliers and is initialized to 0, while the detection output d is initialized to 1. The algorithm alternates between the estimation of the parameters and the detection of a single outlier. Finally, the algorithm returns the scores $\{s_i\}_{i=1}^k$ normalized by the Pareto CDF $H(\cdot, \hat{\kappa}, \hat{\underline{\lambda}})$, which are probabilities between 0 and 1, and the number of outliers n_o in the sorted score list.

Furon and Jégou evaluated Alg. 4.6 over a variety of image retrieval benchmarks. In experiments on the Holidays, Holidays+Flickr1M (Jégou et al. [2010]), University of Kentucky Benchmark (UKB) (Nister and Stewenius [2006]), and Oxford105k (Philbin et al. [2007]) data sets using BOW (Bag of Words), Hamming Embedding and Weak Geometry Consistency (HE+WGC) and GIST descriptors, the proposed approach produced large performance increases over just the consideration of raw scores in all but a single case. When used to normalize the scores of the contextual dissimilarities method of Perronnin et al. [2009], the performance is better or comparable to that of the baseline raw scores, depending on the feature set and distance measure used. The additional computation is reported to have a negligible impact on overall processing time.

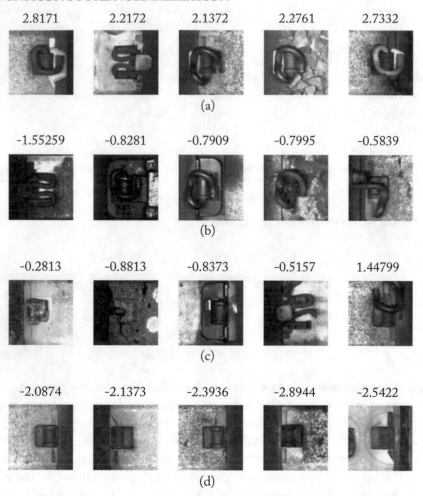

Figure 4.4: A practical application of Pareto-based normalization: railway track inspection (Gibert et al. [2015a]). The recognition scores associated with the quality of rail fasteners can vary widely. This may have serious implications on safety, if defective fasteners have misleadingly high scores. Examples of fastener scores: (a) good fasteners with high scores; (b) good fasteners with low scores; (c) defective fasteners with high scores; and (d) defective fasteners with low scores. Normalization has been shown to reduce the error rate associated defect detection. From Gibert et al. [2015a].

4.4.4 PARETO-BASED NORMALIZATION: VISUAL INSPECTION VIA ANOMALY DETECTION

A different Pareto-based normalization scheme was proposed by Gibert et al. [2015a] for the application of robust railway track inspection (Fig. 4.4). Abnormal conditions on a railway track can have disastrous consequences if not detected and quickly remedied. In an approach similar to that proposed by Broadwater and Chellappa [2010] for hyperspectral and radar target detection, Gibert et al. estimate an adaptive threshold from the GPD fit to the upper tail of the score distribution after removing the outliers using a Kolmogorov-Smirnov statistical test. Key differences from the algorithm of Broadwater and Chellappa [2010] include the use of a Bayesian formulation, operation over sequential data, and the estimation of an adaptive threshold for each sample.

The objective of the algorithm is to adapt the scores of an anomaly detector applied to a sequence of images so that when a given threshold is applied, an expected approximate error rate can be achieved. With respect to the distributional modeling, an important consideration is the choice of window over scores from a process with dynamics that change rapidly. If a GPD is fit to the extreme samples of a short window, the estimated threshold will have too much variance, and will perform worse than if using a fixed threshold. If the window is too long, then the threshold will not adapt at all. One way to address this problem is to fix the shape parameter κ to 0. In this case, the GPD reduces to the exponential distribution:

$$G(y; \lambda, \kappa = 0) = 1 - e^{-y/\lambda}. \tag{4.20}$$

As shorthand notation, let $\phi = 1/\lambda$. The conjugate prior of the exponential distribution is the Gamma distribution:

$$\pi(\phi; \alpha, \beta) = \frac{\beta^\alpha}{\Gamma(\alpha)} \phi^{\alpha-1} e^{-\beta\phi}, \tag{4.21}$$

where the improper prior is given by the parameters $\alpha = 1, \beta = 0$, and the parameters of the Gamma posterior under a Gamma prior Gamma($\phi; \alpha_0, \beta_0$) can be estimated via:

$$\alpha_1 = \alpha_0 + n \tag{4.22}$$

$$\beta_1 = \beta_0 + \sum_{i=1}^{n} y_i. \tag{4.23}$$

Gibert et al. suggest using the following training procedure to find the parameters α_0, β_0 of the gamma prior. First, a training set is assembled with a number of sequences of scores and their corresponding labels. The training process then computes the sufficient statistics (those that are necessary to model the Gamma prior distribution) for all samples that are not labeled as anomalies. These parameters are then rescaled to limit the effect of the Gamma prior. Further, a number of training samples smaller than the size of the entire set is selected to avoid the application of a prior that is too strong, which would bias the resulting Maximum a posteriori estimation (MAP) estimate.

For testing, the algorithm first performs a series of Kolmogorov-Smirnov (KS) tests (Stuart et al. [1999]) to find and remove anomalies. The KS statistic is calculated as:

$$D_n = \sup_x | \widehat{G}_n(x) - G(x; \widehat{\phi}) | \tag{4.24}$$

and measures the dissimilarity between two distributions. $G(x; \widehat{\phi})$ is the GPD and $\widehat{G}_n(x)$ is the empirical CDF of the tail of the score distribution. It is defined as:

$$\widehat{G}_n(x) = 1 - \frac{1}{n} \sum_{i=1}^{n} I(X_i \leq x), \qquad (4.25)$$

where $I(x)$ is an indicator function. An estimated threshold is then used to reject the hypothesis that the observed data does not fit the distribution G. Once the anomalies are culled, the prior estimated during the training stage is used to calculate the posterior for the entire sequence considered in the testing instance. The posterior is subsequently used as the prior for estimating the tail distribution on each shift of a window centered on each sample. Scores are normalized according to this distribution, and then returned for further analysis by the user.

To validate this approach, Gibert et al. considered a data set of Amtrak railway images composed of 340 sequences of fastener detections from 4 cameras in 85 miles of track (Gibert et al. [2015b]). The evaluation task for this data set is to determine whether an image contains a fastener attached to one of the rails. In total, there are 1,087 defects present out of 813,148 images, making the task rather challenging as the objects of interest are rare. In spite of this, the EVT-based normalization in this case leads to a detection rate of 99.26%. For all 813,148 scores derived from the data set, the score normalization takes only 17 s on a 2.5 GHz Intel Core i5 processor.

CHAPTER 5

Calibration of Supervised Machine Learning Algorithms

The general principle of score normalization introduced in Chapter 4 can be applied more directly to supervised machine learning. For many decision-making algorithms, a distance or similarity score is at the heart of their learning objective. The typical training process involves an assessment stage where a feature vector x is classified by the current iteration of a measurable recognition function f, and the resulting score s is checked against the ground-truth label y. When this is the case, the supervised learning process turns out to be highly amenable to *calibration*: the process of mapping raw decision scores to probabilistic decision scores. As we learned earlier in this book, probability scores are desirable for a number of reasons, including putting data on a common basis for fusion and providing the user with more interpretable results from a recognition function. Calibration applies to SVM, Logistic Regression, Random Forests, Boosting, and the Softmax function, among many other algorithms. In this chapter, we will mainly focus on SVM, but we will also take a look at a calibration process for a sparse representation-based classifier, and one for the Softmax function used in conjunction with a convolutional neural network. SVM and Softmax serve as the two most popular readout layers for convolutional neural networks (Fergus [2013]), the current dominant approach to visual recognition.

5.1 GOALS OF CALIBRATION FOR DECISION MAKING

The measurable recognition function f can be a binary classifier, where distance can be assessed from either side of the decision boundary, yielding a distance score s. A threshold δ is applied to s make the final classification decision. If $\delta = 0$, which is common for a binary classifier like SVM, a negative score $-s$ signifies negative classification, and a positive score s signifies positive classification (i.e., the sign is the class label). f could also be a multi-class classifier, typically implemented as an ensemble of binary classifiers, where the same score assessment procedure applies. Let's assume for the moment that we have a basic binary classifier. A number of postulates can be proposed in this scenario.

1. In order to achieve a classification model that is Bayes consistent, conditions must guarantee that the risk of f approach the Bayes risk. Calibration near the decision boundary of a convex solution is one way to induce those conditions. According to Tewari and Bartlett [2007], probability calibration is only well defined close to the decision boundary.

2. The decision boundary is defined by the training samples that are effectively extremes. Consider SVM. Support vectors are a type of extreme sampling that describes the class boundary. In a non-degenerate solution, they are some subset of the entire set of training samples—the points that were most difficult to classify during training. And the entire set of training samples is just a tiny subset of all possible members of a class.

3. If we intend to model a set of extrema for a calibration model, then that calibration model should be based on EVT.

For calibration, the general algorithmic strategy is the following: fit the appropriate EVT distribution to data around the decision boundary to estimate the parameters for one or two models, and then consider scores from the CDF of that model or models to make a decision. There are three possibilities for fitting if the classifier is binary: (1) fitting one distribution to the extrema on the negative side of the decision boundary approaching 0; (2) fitting one distribution to the extrema on the positive side of the decision boundary approaching 0; and (3) fitting two distributions to extrema on both sides of the decision boundary approaching zero. In the rest of this chapter, we will look at all of these possibilities as they apply to SVM and Softmax, and a variety of visual recognition problems.

5.2   PROBABILITY OF EXCLUSION: MULTI-ATTRIBUTE SPACES

The multi-attribute spaces algorithm (Scheirer et al. [2012a]) fits a Weibull distribution to the extrema on the positive *or* negative side of the decision boundary approaching zero (the first and second scenarios described in Sec. 5.1). The resulting model helps us estimate the probability of exclusion, i.e., the probability of a sample not being drawn from the decision space opposite the one we're interested in. While originally designed to address the problem of combining different describable visual attribute classifiers (e.g., classifiers that assign scores for gender, hair color, eye color, various object textures), multi-attribute spaces can be viewed as a general strategy for the calibration of binary classifiers. When it is used for attribute fusion, however, the objective is to create a uniform interpretation of scores across classifiers, where distances between points in the normalized space correspond to perceptual similarity between images. The goal is better multi-attribute search results compared to uncalibrated classifiers, and similarity searches based on target attributes, defined using a given query image.

The calibration process is detailed in Alg. 5.7. More formally, given an input feature vector x, an SVM f outputs a score s. As described earlier, the sign of s usually determines its class—positive or negative. In the multi-attribute spaces algorithm, however, s is calibrated by fitting a Weibull distribution $W(\kappa, \lambda)$ to the extreme values of the distribution for the side of the decision boundary opposite to the one we are interested in. For attribute classifiers, this means the model could apply to both sides (e.g., for a gender classifier, where "male" and "female" are valid outcomes; Fig. 5.1), or just one side (e.g., a specific hair color classifier like "blonde"). The

---

Algorithm 5.7 EVT normalization of binary SVM decision scores

---

Require: A vector of decision scores $S = \{s_i\}$, of length m, from a single binary SVM classifier

Require: n, the number of elements used for fitting

1: **Let** $V \subset S$ be scores from the opposite decision space
2: **if** the negative decision space is chosen **then**
3:     $\phi = 1$
4: **else**
5:     $\phi = -1$
6: **end if**
7: $\hat{V} = \phi * V$ # If needed, flip so extrema are largest
8: **Sort** $\hat{V}$ retaining n largest scores: $D = d_n > \ldots > d_1$
9: Let $\hat{D} = D - d_1 + 1$ # Shift to be positive
10: **Fit** a Weibull distribution W to $\hat{D}$
11: Let $T(x) = \phi * x - d_1 + 1$;
12: **for** $i = 1 \rightarrow m$ **do**
13:     $s_i' = F(T(s_i); W)$
14: **end for**
15: **return** normalized decision scores $\{s_i'\}$

---

algorithm first applies a transform T that flips and shifts these scores as needed to satisfy two conditions that are necessary for this formulation: the data must always be positive, regardless of the side of the decision boundary we are considering, and that the extreme values must be the largest scores in the set of scores. After this, a Weibull distribution W is fit to the transformed scores, and each score is normalized using the CDF F defined by the parameters of the model W: $F(T(s_i); W)$. Note that ground truth data is not necessary for this process (assuming the SVMs have already been trained using appropriate data). With respect to an implementation of multi-attribute spaces, it is essentially the same exact process as the w-score algorithm from Sec. 4.2, with the statistical fitting functionality provided by the libMR library. The only difference is the score transformation process in lines 7–9 and 11 of Alg. 5.7.

How good is this algorithm in practice? Through extensive experiments on a large data set of almost 2 million faces, Scheirer et al. [2012a] showed that this principled probabilistic approach to score normalization greatly improves the accuracy and utility of face retrieval using multi-attribute searches, and allows for the new capability of performing similarity searches based on target attributes in query images. For quantitative evaluation, 30 different textual queries (e.g., "white babies wearing hats") were generated, sampling from combinations of 42 different attributes, and side-by-side top 10 face retrieval results for multi-attribute spaces and the describable visual attributes approach of Kumar et al. [2011] were submitted to 30 different Mechanical Turk workers (order and side were randomized per test to remove presentation bias). For all 30

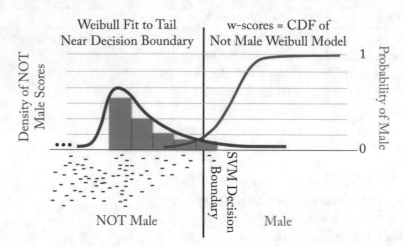

Figure 5.1: A one-sided calibration method for decision boundaries that models the probability of exclusion: multi-attributes spaces (Scheirer et al. [2012a]). It was originally proposed for describable visual attributes (Kumar et al. [2011]), but is extendable to general decision-making algorithms (Jain et al. [2014], Scheirer et al. [2014a]). SVM decision scores are normalized by fitting a Weibull distribution (the red curve) to the tail of the opposite side of the classifier via the w-score process we discussed in Chapter 4, where instances of the attribute of interest ("male" in this case) are outliers. The CDF of this distribution (the blue curve) is used to produce the normalized attribute w-scores. Note that no assumptions are made about the entire score distribution (which can vary greatly); the model is applied to only the tail of the distribution, which is much better behaved. Based on Scheirer et al. [2012a].

queries, each worker was asked to identify the set of results that was more relevant, yielding 900 individual comparisons. The null hypothesis in this case indicates equal votes for each algorithm for each query, which was evaluated with a one-sided paired t-test. The results from the multi-attribute spaces approach were chosen as "more relevant" by the workers for the given queries 86.9% of the time.

5.3   OPEN SET RECOGNITION

More interesting perhaps than closed set recognition problems like attribute assignment are *open set* recognition problems, where unknown classes must be expected as input to a given classifier. These problems lie at the heart visual recognition, and must be addressed if one is to solve the general scene understanding problem. Recent classification results reported for the ImagetNet Large Scale Visual Recognition Challenge 2015 [ILSVRC2015] have captured the computer vision community's interest. For classification tasks 2a (classification + localization with provided training data) and 2b (classification + localization with additional training data) of the 2015 Im-

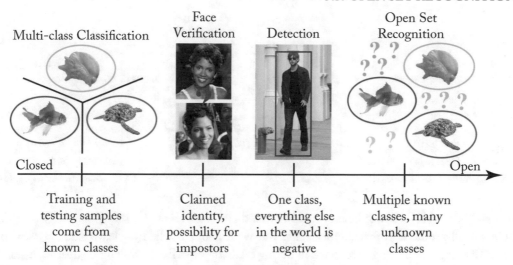

Figure 5.2: Recognition problems arranged in increasing levels of "openness." On one extreme is the familiar problem of closed set recognition in computer vision, where only classes seen at training time are evaluated at testing time. Most benchmark data sets are organized in this manner, from classic sets like MNIST (LeCun et al. [1998]) to state-of-the-art challenges like ImageNet Classification (Russakovsky et al. [2015]). However, there are other familiar problems like face verification and detection that must manage unknown inputs at testing time. But even these problems are somewhat tractable with binary classifiers that have a negative decision space that can reject inputs. For more comprehensive scene understanding, we need to solve the *open set recognition problem*, where multiple known classes and a practically infinite number of unknown classes may be present. Supervised learning algorithms with EVT-based calibration can help us in each of these cases. From Scheirer et al. [2013].

ageNet challenge, error rates of 3.6% and 4.6% were, respectively, achieved. With such low error rates, one might believe that we are closer to solving real-world visual object recognition than ever before. However, it is fair to ask if a scenario in which all classes are known during training time leads to an accurate assessment of the overall state of object recognition. Importantly, the detection results from the 2015 ImageNet challenge tell a different story. When unknown objects must be rejected in the process of detecting the location and label of a known object, no approach produces a result as impressive as what we see for classification: the best results were a mean average precision of just 62.1% for task 1a (object detection with provided training data) and 57.8% for task 1b (object detection with additional training data). Detection falls under the general class of machine learning problems known as open set recognition (Scheirer et al. [2013]), i.e., when the possibility of encountering novel classes not present in training exists during testing.

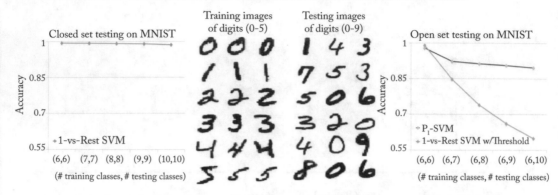

Figure 5.3: The MNIST database of handwritten digits (LeCun et al. [1998]) is widely considered to be a solved problem in machine learning. But what happens when we leave some classes out at training time and then bring them back in during testing? (First Panel) Standard supervised learning algorithms approach ceiling on the original MNIST classification problem. Shown are results for a 1-vs-Rest SVM with Platt [2000] probability estimates using the same number of training and testing classes, where all classes are seen during training. (Second Panel) Training data consisting of six classes from MNIST. (Third Panel) Testing data consisting of all ten classes from MNIST, including four classes unseen during training. (Fourth Panel) By changing the testing regime to a process where some number of classes are held out during training but included in testing, MNIST once again becomes a challenge. As soon as classes are withheld during training, the accuracy of the 1-vs-Rest SVM (with a rejection option provided by thresholding the Platt probability estimates) drops significantly. What we'd like is an algorithm with behavior like the P_I-SVM (described in Sec. 5.3.1), which retains higher levels of accuracy as the problem grows to be more open. From Jain et al. [2014].

After moving to the open set multi-class recognition scenario, even what appear to be very simple "solved" pattern recognition tasks become quite difficult. To illustrate this often surprising point, Fig. 5.3 demonstrates what happens when a classic closed set classification problem such as the MNIST database of handwritten digits (LeCun et al. [1998]) is transformed into a challenging multi-class open set recognition problem. Note the remarkable drop in performance for the off-the-shelf 1-vs-Rest SVM with a threshold as classes not seen at training time are encountered at testing time. Several classification algorithms show potential for open set recognition problems, including exemplar SVM (Malisiewicz et al. [2011]), which trains on a single positive example and millions of negative examples to achieve surprisingly good generalization, and hybrid models (Lasserre et al. [2006]) that incorporate a generative component to account for impoverished labeled training regimes. A more direct way (Fumera and Roli [2002], Kwok [1999], Zhang and Metaxas [2006]) to approach the multi-class open set recognition problem is to incorporate a posterior probability estimator $P(y|x)$, where $y \in \mathbb{N}$ is a class label and $x \in \mathbb{R}^d$ is multi-dimensional feature data, and a decision threshold into an existing multi-class algorithm.

Letting $\mathcal{C}$ be the set of known classes, testing is a two step process: (1) compute the maximum probability over known classes, and (2) label the data as "unknown" if that probability is below the threshold δ:

$$y^* = \begin{cases} \text{argmax}_{y_i \in \mathcal{C}} \, P(y_i | x) & \text{if } P(y^* | x) \geq \delta \\ \text{"unknown"} & \text{Otherwise.} \end{cases} \qquad (5.1)$$

Such a thresholded probability model can support a multi-class classifier with a rejection option, e.g., the 1-vs-Rest SVM with a threshold applied over Platt [2000] calibrated decision scores as shown in Fig. 5.3d. A key question when applying any probability estimator is: how do we build a consistent probability model without over-fitting or over-generalizing? While better than a strict multi-class SVM, which always assigns a known class label, SVM with a rejection option is still not very good for open set recognition. It is weak because it implicitly makes closed set assumptions during the decision score calibration process. In open set recognition, a sample that is not from a known negative class does not necessarily imply that it is from the positive class. Furthermore, because we must consider the possibility of unknown classes, Bayes' theorem does not directly apply. The best we can do is produce an unnormalized posterior estimate. In essence, we need a good way, in an open class setting, to consistently estimate the unnormalized posterior probability of inclusion for each class. This is what we will look at next.

5.3.1 PROBABILITY OF INCLUSION: P_I-SVM

Intuitively, a one-class classifier like the one-class SVM (Schölkopf et al. [2001]) should be able to solve the open set recognition problem, because no prior knowledge of any negative class is needed during training. With a model of just the class of interest, it is in principle possible to reject any unknown input submitted to the classifier. Unfortunately, it is well established that one-class classifiers tend to aggressively overfit their training data (Zhou and Huang [2003]). Thus we seek an approach for probability estimation that combines the ability to discriminate between known classes like a binary classifier, but with one-class-like rejection ability. To model this, the probability of inclusion, we only consider scores from the binary classifier that are associated with training data samples from a single class of interest in modeling. But what probability model should we use?

As shown by Bartlett and Tewari [2007], for any $\zeta \in (1/2, 1)$ one can accurately estimate conditional probabilities in the interval $(1 - \zeta, \zeta)$ only if support vectors are not sparse over that interval. For efficient classifiers we need some degree of sparsity, thus ζ should be close to $1/2$ and probability calibration is only well defined close to the decision boundary. And since that boundary is defined by the training samples that are effectively extremes, we conclude that proper models for efficient SVM calibration should be based on EVT. Different from the multi-attribute spaces algorithm that applied EVT via rejection of a hypothesis, the P_I-SVM (Jain et al. [2014]) uses EVT to directly model probability of inclusion for a class of interest.

Algorithm 5.8 Multi-class EVT-based probability modeling for P_I-SVM training

---

Require: A set of class labels C; a set of labeled training data points for each class $X_y, y \in C$; a pre-trained 1-vs-Rest RBF SVM h_y for each class $y \in C$, with positive support vectors α_y^+;

1: **for** $y = 1 \rightarrow |C|$ **do**
2:     **for** $j = 1 \rightarrow |X_y|$ **do**
3:         $s_{y,j} = h_y(x_{y,j})$
4:         **if** $s_{y,j} > 0$ **then**
5:             $\mathcal{M}_y = \mathcal{M}_y \cup \{s_{y,j}\}$
6:         **end if**
7:     **end for**
8:     $p_y = 1.5 * |\alpha_y^+|$ # tail estimation strategy from Sec. 2.4
9:     Sort $\mathcal{M}_y$ retaining p_y smallest items as vector ℓ_y
10:     $[\tau_y, \kappa_y, \lambda_y] = \text{wblfit}(\ell_y)$
11:     $\theta_y = [\tau_y, \kappa_y, \lambda_y]$
12: **end for**
13:
14: **return** $\mathcal{W} = [\theta_1 \ldots \theta_{|C|}]$

The basis of the P_I-SVM is a a kernelized SVM h that for any d-dimensional feature vector x will generate an uncalibrated hypothesis score s, which can be used to assign class membership:

$$h(x) = \sum_{i=1}^{n} y_i \alpha_i K(x_i, x) + b, \tag{5.2}$$

where α_i are support vectors, $K(x_i, x)$ is a radial basis function kernel, and b a bias term. A collection of such binary classifiers for each class $y \in C$ forms a multi-class SVM. For an uncalibrated SVM hypothesis score $s = h_y(x), s > 0$ it can be assumed that larger scores imply more likely inclusion in class y. Given the nature of the SVM decision boundary, such inclusion scores are bounded from below, though it is straightforward to adapt the model to unbounded scores, depending on the desired EVT distribution for probability estimation.

Now consider a multi-class problem for the known training classes C where it is not assumed that the list of classes is exhaustive, i.e., the open set recognition problem. The objective of the P_I-SVM is to compute a per class unnormalized posterior probability estimate for any input sample x. For P_I-SVM training, let $\{(x_1, y), (x_2, y), \ldots, (x_n, y)\}$ be a collection of training samples that will be used to fit a probability estimator for a single class. Let the overall match set be represented by $\mathcal{M}_y$, with $s_j \in \mathcal{M}_y$ if $h_y(x_j) > 0$. Let ℓ_y be the lower extremes of $\mathcal{M}_y$ (for SVM, the scores closest to 0). With a set of scores bounded from below, the correct EVT distribution to model ℓ_y is the Weibull. Algorithm 5.8 provides a precise description of the Weibull probability modeling of class inclusion for each of the classes present during P_I-SVM training.

After fitting, the probability model of inclusion defined by a set of parameters θ_y can be used as a robust probability estimator for a classifier. Let $\rho(y)$ be the prior probability of class y. Then the posterior probability of inclusion P_I can be estimated for the input x and class label y conditioned on the parameters θ_y as:

$$P_I(y|x, \theta_y) = \xi\rho(y)P_I(x|y, \theta_y) = \xi\rho(y)(1 - e^{-(\frac{x-\tau_y}{\lambda_y})^{\kappa_y}}) \tag{5.3}$$

for some constant ξ. If all classes and priors are known, then Bayes' Theorem yields

$$\xi = \frac{1}{\sum_{y\in C}\rho(y)P_I(x|y, \theta_y)}. \tag{5.4}$$

Because we are interested in open set recognition, it is not assumed that all classes are known, so $\xi = 1$ and the posterior estimate is treated as *unnormalized*. The use of unnormalized posterior estimation is useful because as long as the missing normalization constant is consistent across all classes it still allows the use of maximum *a posteriori* estimation. Note that unnormalized posterior probabilities are always an approximation; the unknown constant ξ could be very large or very small which changes the true probability.

For multi-class open set recognition using a set of Weibull models, we place a minimum threshold δ on class probability and select

$$y^* = \underset{y\in C}{\mathrm{argmax}}\, P_I(y|x, \theta_y) \quad \text{subject to} \quad P_I(y^*|x, \theta_{y^*}) \geq \delta. \tag{5.5}$$

The formulation in Eq. 5.5 yields the most likely class, which is appropriate if the classes are exclusive. Alternatively, if the classes are overlapping, one might return all classes above a given probability threshold. Note that we are dealing with unnormalized posterior estimations so the priors $\rho(y)$ only need to be relatively scaled, e.g., they could sum to one even if there are unknown classes. It has been shown by Chow [1970] that the optimal value for the threshold is a function of the risk associated with making a correct decision, making an error, or making a rejection, respectively, as well as the prior probabilities of the known or unknown classes. In practice, these would come from the domain knowledge. One can also simply assume equal priors per class; accordingly, δ would be set to the prior probability of an unknown instance. Algorithm 5.9 describes the P_I-SVM probability estimation process for a new test sample. The estimate for probability of inclusion $P_I(x|y, \theta_y)$ comes from the CDF of the Weibull model defined by the parameters θ_y (see the right-hand side of Eq. 5.3).

The P_I-SVM algorithm is implemented as part of the libsvm-openset package, available on github (`https://github.com/ljain2/libsvm-openset`). libsvm-openset is a patched version of the popular libsvm package (Chang and Lin [2011]), which implements a variety of SVM variants. Installation involves two steps: building and installing libMR (which we have already used throughout this book), and building libsvm-openset. Build instructions are provided in the `README-libsvm-openset` file included in the libsvm-openset repository. In the following examples, we will train and test a P_I-SVM, and demonstrate the effect of thresholding probability

---

Algorithm 5.9 Multi-class probability estimation for P_I-SVM testing

---

Require: A set of class labels $\mathcal{C}$; a pre-trained 1-vs-Rest RBF SVM h_y for each class y; parameter set $\mathcal{W}$ from Alg. 5.8; probability threshold δ for rejection; class prior probability $\rho(y)$ for each class y; a test sample x

1: $y^* =$ "unknown"
2: $\omega = 0$
3: **for** $y = 1 \rightarrow |\mathcal{C}|$ **do**
4:    $P_I(x|y, \theta_y) = \text{wblcdf}(x, \theta_y)$
5:    $P_I(y|x, \theta_y) = \rho(y) P_I(x|y, \theta_y)$
6:    **if** $P_I(y|x, \theta_y) > \delta$ **then**
7:       **if** $P_I(y|x, \theta_y) > \omega$ **then**
8:          $y^* = y$
9:          $\omega = P_I(y|x, \theta_y)$
10:      **end if**
11:   **end if**
12: **end for**
13:
14: **return** $[y^*, \omega]$

---

scores. The data set we will consider is an open set partition of MNIST (LeCun et al. [1998]), which can be downloaded from the following URL: http://www.wjscheirer.com/misc/EV TMVR/data/. The training file mnist.scale.3 contains feature vectors for three distinct classes ("0", "1", "2") in libsvm format. The testing file mnist.scale.t.openset contains all of the MNIST testing vectors for the complete ten classes, with the training classes tagged with their corresponding labels, and the remaining unknown classes labeled with "-1". All features have been scaled to fall between the range 0–1 for faster processing by the algorithm.

To train a P_I-SVM, the svm-train program should be invoked with the flag -s 10, along with the path to a training file. Let's also set the flag -c 1000, which leads to what is in effect a hard margin SVM. The RBF kernel parameter γ can also be set, but we will use the libsvm default of 1/num_features here. The output of the training process is shown below. Note that the statistical fitting procedure is invoked for each class, giving us three sets of Weibull parameters for the three training rounds.

```
$ ./svm-train -c 1000 -s 10 ./data/mnist.scale.3
Training binary 1-vs-set for class 0 with 5923 pos and 12700 neg
examples
...*...*
optimization finished, #iter = 6513
nu = 0.000847
```

```
obj = -7886.210306, rho = 6.585513
nSV = 365, nBSV = 0
Total nSV = 365
Training binary 1-vs-set for class 1 with 6742 pos and 11881 neg
examples
.....*...*
optimization finished, #iter = 8554
nu = 0.001416
obj = -13185.426341, rho = -9.456788
nSV = 378, nBSV = 0
Total nSV = 378
Training binary 1-vs-set for class 2 with 5958 pos and 12665 neg
examples
.............*.........*
optimization finished, #iter = 21910
nu = 0.003213
obj = -30143.758877, rho = 16.469464
nSV = 747, nBSV = 1
Total nSV = 747
Total nSV = 1490
```

After training, a model file `mnist.scale.3.model` will be available for use as a classifier in conjunction with the `svm-predict` program, which also expects the paths to a testing file and output file. The `-P` flag is used to set the probability threshold for class membership. Let's consider a range of probabilities (0.0, 0.25, 0.5, 0.75, 0.95) and run `svm-predict` with each one:

```
$ ./svm-predict -P 0.0 ./data/mnist.scale.t.openset
  mnist.scale.3.model outfile
Recognition Accuracy = 30.75%
Precision=0.309730, Recall=0.977121 Fmeasure=0.470363
Total tests=10000, True pos 3075 True Neg 0, False Pos 6853,
False neg 72

$ ./svm-predict -P 0.25 ./data/mnist.scale.t.openset
  mnist.scale.3.model outfile
Recognition Accuracy = 72.9%
Precision=0.538817, Recall=0.963775 Fmeasure=0.691203
Total tests=10000, True pos 3033 True Neg 4257, False Pos 2596,
False neg 114
```

```
$ ./svm-predict -P 0.5 ./data/mnist.scale.t.openset
  mnist.scale.3.model outfile
Recognition Accuracy = 74.27%
Precision=0.552391, Recall=0.961551 Fmeasure=0.701681
Total tests=10000, True pos 3026 True Neg 4401, False Pos 2452,
False neg 121


$ ./svm-predict -P 0.75 ./data/mnist.scale.t.openset
  mnist.scale.3.model outfile
Recognition Accuracy = 75.72%
Precision=0.567792, Recall=0.956784 Fmeasure=0.712663
Total tests=10000, True pos 3011 True Neg 4561, False Pos 2292,
False neg 136


$ ./svm-predict -P 0.95 ./data/mnist.scale.t.openset
  mnist.scale.3.model outfile
Recognition Accuracy = 78.45%
Precision=0.599598, Recall=0.948840 Fmeasure=0.734835
Total tests=10000, True pos 2986 True Neg 4859, False Pos 1994,
False neg 161
```

Unpacking the above output, we see that svm-predict returns a variety of statistics, including overall recognition accuracy (i.e., how many testing vectors were correctly classified), the information retrieval statistics of precision, recall and F-measure, and the breakdown of each classification decision into the categories of true positive, true negative, false positive and false negative. With a threshold of 0.0, only scores exceeding this absolute baseline will be considered members of one of the positive classes. While recall in this case is truly excellent, accuracy and precision are quite low, because the negative samples are misclassified as positive samples. As we increase the threshold, accuracy and precision go up, while recall remains fairly stable. When the probability threshold reaches 0.95, accuracy hits a high point of 78.45% for this test, but at the expense of an increasing number of false negatives—there is some tradeoff between reducing false positives and increasing true positives. Nevertheless, the probability thresholds give us a convenient tool for controlling the decision boundary in an interpretable score space—all thanks to the calibration inherent in the P_I-SVM.

A more comprehensive version of the open set MNIST benchmark was used by Jain et al. [2014] to compare the P_I-SVM to a number of different classifiers, including the multi-attribute spaces algorithm, 1-vs-Rest multi-class SVM with a threshold, pairwise multi-class SVM with a threshold, and logistic regression with a threshold. In all cases, the P_I-SVM was shown to achieve a higher F-measure score than all other algorithms. Similarly, an open set LETTER

(Michie et al. [1994]) benchmark with 26 total classes was used by Jain et al., with the P_I-SVM again achieving the highest F-measures across the various comparison algorithms. But, of course, even these more challenging versions of the MNIST and LETTER data sets aren't considered to be state-of-the-art visual recognition benchmarks. To address this, Jain et al. evaluated the P_I-SVM on an open set object detection task for an open universe of 88 classes, where images from Caltech 256 were used for training and images from Caltech 256 and ImageNet were used for testing. As with the other experiments, the P_I-SVM was shown to be superior in F-measure to all comparison approaches.

5.3.2   PROBABILITY OF INCLUSION AND EXCLUSION: W-SVM

Both the multi-attribute spaces and P_I-SVM algorithms fit a distribution to one side of the decision boundary of a binary classifier. A more powerful probabilistic formulation turns out to be fitting two distributions to extrema on both sides of the decision boundary. Out of all of the existing EVT-based calibration methods, the current best performing algorithm for open set recognition problems is the W-SVM (Scheirer et al. [2014a]), a Weibull-calibrated formulation that combines a one-class SVM with a binary SVM, both with non-linear kernels. Why does such an algorithm help address the open set recognition problem? First, when Weibull modeling is coupled with a one-class SVM using a radial basis function kernel, it can be proved that the probability of class membership decreases in value as points move from known data toward open space (see Sec. III of Scheirer et al. [2014a]). This effect leads to a Compact Abating Probability (CAP) model. Second, the Weibull distribution provides better modeling at the decision boundaries for a binary SVM, resulting in good generalization even in the presence of many unknown classes. The W-SVM ensures that the probability models do not treat data at the decision boundaries as low probability members of a class, where separation between different classes in a raw distance sense may be small.

The W-SVM training algorithm consists of four distinct steps split into two different classification regimes: one-class and binary. The base formulation applies to multi-class classification problems and binary classification problems. Given the more complicated nature of this algorithm compared to the others we have looked at in this chapter, the complete training process is described visually in Fig. 5.4.

Algorithm 5.10 provides a more precise description of the W-SVM EVT probability modeling for each of the k classes considered in multi-class recognition. Each class y_i in the multi-class problem is represented individually as the combination of a one-class RBF SVM and a 1-vs-All binary RBF SVM. It can be assumed that all of the individual one-class SVMs and 1-vs-All binary SVMs have been trained in advance. Note that Alg. 5.10 makes use (and refers to) functions in the libMR library, which provides the underlying statistical estimation functionality in the implementation we will discuss below.

Open set recognition is a primary consideration of Alg. 5.10. As with all of the EVT-based algorithms we've looked at, a key question that needs to be addressed is the size of the tail for

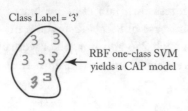

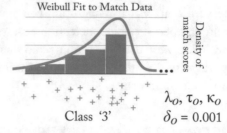

Step 1. Train a One-class SVM f^o Step 2. Fit Weibull Distribution Over Tail of Scores from f^o

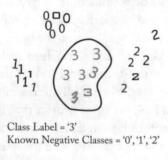

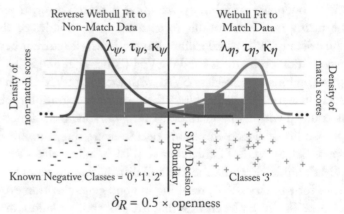

Step 3. Train a Binary RBF SVM f Step 4. Fit EVT Distribution Over Tails of Scores from f

Figure 5.4: W-SVM Training. For simplicity, the procedure is shown for a single class (the same steps are repeated for k known classes during training). In steps 1 and 2, a one-class SVM f^o is trained and a Weibull distribution is fit to the corresponding tail of scores from that SVM for samples of data known at training time. This yields a Weibull model of the data with parameters $\lambda_o, \tau_o, \kappa_o$. The one-class probability threshold δ_o is set to 0.001. In steps 3 and 4, a binary SVM f is trained and two EVT distributions are fit to the corresponding scores from that SVM for samples of data known at training time. A Reverse Weibull distribution is fit to the tail of the non-match data (scores for known classes other than '3'), yielding a model with parameters $\lambda_\psi, \tau_\psi, \kappa_\psi$. A Weibull distribution is fit to the tail of the match data (scores for class '3'), yielding a model with parameters $\lambda_\eta, \tau_\eta, \kappa_\eta$. A rejection threshold δ_R is set for the overall W-SVM to $0.5 \times$ openness (see Eq. 5.6 for a definition of openness). The collection of SVM models, EVT distribution parameters, and thresholds constitute the W-SVM.

Algorithm 5.10 W-SVM multi-class model fitting

Require:

Classes $y_i, i = 1 \rightarrow k$;

Pre-trained 1-vs-All binary SVM for each class y_i, with score functions f_i and support vectors α_i^-, α_i^+;

Pre-trained one-class SVM for each class y_i, with score functions f_i^o and support vectors α_i^o;

Labeled training data X_i;

Tail size multiplier $\theta = 0.5$ for detection, or $\theta = 1.5$ for multi-class recognition

1-vs-all binary SVM scores $s_{i,j} = f_i(x_j), x_j \in X_i$;

One-class SVM scores $o_{i,j} = f_i^o(x_j), x_j \in X_i$;

Meta-Recognition object MR from libMR, providing MLE-based Weibull fitting and score calibration.

1: **for** $i = 1 \rightarrow k$ **do**
2:     1. Let $q_i^+ = \theta \times |\alpha_i^+|, q_i^- = \theta \times |\alpha_i^-|, q_i^o = \theta \times |\alpha_i^o|$
3:     2. Let d_i^- be the set of binary non-match scores: $s_{i,j} = f_i(x_j)$ when x_j does not belong to y_i
4:     3. Let d_i^+ be the set of binary match scores: $s_{i,j} = f_i(x_j)$ when x_j belongs to y_i
5:     4. Let d_i^o be the set of one-class scores: $o_{i,j} = f_i^o(x_j)$ when x_j belongs to y_i
6:     5. Let $[\tau_{\psi,i}, \lambda_{\psi,i}, \kappa_{\psi,i}] =$
       MR.fitSVM(d_i^-, y_i, false, MetaRecognition::complement_model, q_i^+)
7:     6. Let $[\tau_{\eta,i}, \lambda_{\eta,i}, \kappa_{\eta,i}] =$ MR.fitSVM(d_i^+, y_i, true, MetaRecognition::positive_model, q_i^-)
8:     7. Let $[\tau_{o,i}, \lambda_{o,i}, \kappa_{o,i}] =$ MR.fitSVM(d_i^o, y_i, false, MetaRecognition::positive_model, q_i^o)
9: **end for**
10:
11: **return** $\mathcal{W} = [\tau_{\eta,i}, \lambda_{\eta,i}, \kappa_{\eta,i}, \tau_{\psi,i}, \lambda_{\psi,i}, \kappa_{\psi,i}, \tau_{o,i}, \lambda_{o,i}, \kappa_{o,i}]$

---

fitting. In an open set context, this question can be partially answered by considering the notion of problem *openness*. Openness, as introduced by Scheirer et al. [2013] is defined as

$$\text{openness} = 1 - \sqrt{(2 \times \mathcal{C}_T / (\mathcal{C}_R + \mathcal{C}_E))}, \tag{5.6}$$

where $\mathcal{C}_R$ is the number of classes to be recognized, $\mathcal{C}_T$ the number of classes in training, and $\mathcal{C}_E$ the number of classes in testing. The tail size q_i (number of extrema) is estimated based on the number of support vectors for the associated SVMs. This could be 0.5 times the number of support vectors for a detection task, which has very high openness and hence needs strong rejection, or 1.5 times the number of support vectors for a multi-class recognition task, which is more permissive at a lower level of openness.

For the binary SVMs, parameters are estimated for both the non-match (where a Reverse Weibull is used for the fitting) and the match (where a Weibull is used for the fitting) distributions.

Note that in doing so, the match data for one class will be considered non-match data for another. The sets of decision scores d_i^-, d_i^+ and d_i^o are collected from the non-match and the match scores for class y_i. libMR is then used to compute the parameters. The match scores are effectively transformed in the library, so that larger values are the points closer to the margin.

In steps 5, 6 and 7, calls are made to the library function FitSVM to estimate the Reverse Weibull or Weibull parameters. The first parameter is the set of scores, the second is the class label, the third indicates if the class of interest should have positive scores, the fourth is a self-evident enum indicating the type of model, and the fifth is the tail size to use in fitting.

The complete testing process for a known and unknown input is described visually in Figs. 5.5 and 5.6. Algorithm 5.11 gives the description of the W-SVM probability estimation for a new test sample. The function computes an indicator variable ι based on the probability from the one-class model, and the probability of inclusion P_ι and probability of exclusion P_ε (recall Sec. 1.3) from the binary model for each class. Given these values one can use the following expression to make a final decision:

$$y^* = \underset{y \in \mathcal{Y}}{\operatorname{argmax}} \, P_{\eta,y}(x) \times P_{\psi,y}(x) \times \iota_y \tag{5.7}$$
$$\text{subject to } P_{\eta,y^*}(x) \times P_{\psi,y^*}(x) \geq \delta_R.$$

The W-SVM has two parameters: δ_o, which is generally very small (e.g., 0.001) and is used to adjust what data the one-class SVM considers to be even remotely related and determines whether or not ι_y is set, and δ_R, which is the level of confidence needed in the W-SVM estimate itself. In terms of computational costs, the EVT fittings and probability estimations are very fast, taking only milliseconds for each sample. Compared to using Platt-style sigmoids and cross-validation for parameter estimation, the W-SVM is much faster.

The `libsvm-openset` program also contains functionality for the W-SVM algorithm. Its usage is very similar to that of the P_I-SVM, with the difference of the specification of the `-s 8` flag. To demonstrate this algorithm, we again we turn to the open set partition of the MNIST data set, which we used above to demonstrate the P_I-SVM. By default the W-SVM algorithm will use an RBF kernel, which ensures that the resulting classifier will include a CAP model, making it a better solution for open set recognition. The RBF kernel parameter γ can also be set, but again we will use the libsvm default of 1/num_features here.

```
$ ./svm-train -s 8 ./data/mnist.scale.3
Training binary 1-vs-rest WSVM for class 0 with 5923 pos and 12700 neg
examples
*
optimization finished, #iter = 779
nu = 0.049335
obj = -664.480880, rho = 0.723621
nSV = 962, nBSV = 877
```

```
Total nSV = 962
Training binary 1-vs-rest WSVM for class 1 with 6742 pos and 11881 neg
examples
*
optimization finished, #iter = 697
nu = 0.050149
obj = -681.083126, rho = 2.494896
nSV = 966, nBSV = 908
Total nSV = 966
Training binary 1-vs-rest WSVM for class 2 with 5958 pos and 12665 neg
examples
.
Warning: using -h 0 may be faster
*
optimization finished, #iter = 1666
nu = 0.115447
obj = -1613.016037, rho = 1.567850
nSV = 2209, nBSV = 2096
Total nSV = 2209
Total nSV = 4137
CAP-WSVM model
Building one-class model with 5923 pos for class 0
.*
optimization finished, #iter = 1491
obj = 3760338.045214, rho = 2564.797285
nSV = 2966, nBSV = 2958
Building one-class model with 6742 pos for class 1
.*
optimization finished, #iter = 1673
obj = 5271924.098833, rho = 3156.331991
nSV = 3372, nBSV = 3370
Building one-class model with 5958 pos for class 2
.*
optimization finished, #iter = 1471
obj = 3800663.782286, rho = 2576.685783
nSV = 2983, nBSV = 2976
Total nSV = 9321
```

Step 1. Apply One-class SVM CAP
Model for All Known Classes

Input: x = $\mathbf{3}$
$f_0^o(x) = s_0 \quad f_1^o(x) = s_1$
$f_2^o(x) = s_2 \quad f_3^o(x) = s_3$

Step 2. Normalize All One-class SVM Scores
Using EVT Models

$\lambda_{o,0}, \tau_{o,0}, \kappa_{o,0}$
s_0

$\lambda_{o,1}, \tau_{o,1}, \kappa_{o,1}$
s_1

Apply CDF for each class to each score ⟶

$\lambda_{o,2}, \tau_{o,2}, \kappa_{o,2}$
s_2

$\lambda_{o,3}, \tau_{o,3}, \kappa_{o,3}$
s_3

Probability model for test instance: P_O

Step 3. Test Probabilities

$P_o(0|x) < \delta_o, \iota_0 = 0; \quad P_o(1|x) < \delta_o, \iota_1 = 0;$
$P_o(2|x) > \delta_o, \iota_2 = 0; \quad P_o(3|x) > \delta_o, \iota_3 = 0;$

Step 4. Apply Binary SVMs

$f_2(x) = s_2 \quad f_3(x) = s_3$

Step 5. Normalize all Binary SVM Scores
Using EVT Match and Non-match Models

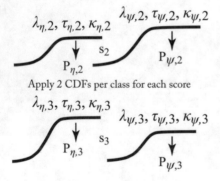

$\lambda_{\eta,2}, \tau_{\eta,2}, \kappa_{\eta,2}$
s_2
$P_{\eta,2}$

$\lambda_{\psi,2}, \tau_{\psi,2}, \kappa_{\psi,2}$
$P_{\psi,2}$

Apply 2 CDFs per class for each score

$\lambda_{\eta,3}, \tau_{\eta,3}, \kappa_{\eta,3}$
s_3
$P_{\eta,3}$

$\lambda_{\psi,3}, \tau_{\psi,3}, \kappa_{\psi,3}$
$P_{\psi,3}$

Step 6. Fuse and Test Probabilities

$P_{\eta,0}(x) \times P_{\psi,0}(x) \times \iota_0 = 0 < \delta_R$
$P_{\eta,1}(x) \times P_{\psi,1}(x) \times \iota_1 = 0 < \delta_R$
$P_{\eta,2}(x) \times P_{\psi,2}(x) \times \iota_2 = 0.001 < \delta_R$
$P_{\eta,3}(x) \times P_{\psi,3}(x) \times \iota_3 = 0.877 > \delta_R$

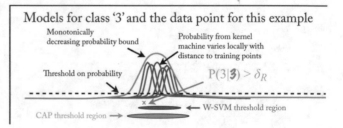

Models for class '3' and the data point for this example

Monotonically decreasing probability bound

Probability from kernel machine varies locally with distance to training points

Threshold on probability

$P(3|\mathbf{3}) > \delta_R$

CAP threshold region ⟶   ⟵ W-SVM threshold region

Figure 5.5: W-SVM testing when the input comes from a known class ('3'). Classes marked in red indicate rejection, and those marked in green indicate acceptance. The first stage of the algorithm (steps 1–3) applies the one-class SVM CAP models from each class to the input data, normalizes the resulting scores to probabilities, and then tests each probability against the threshold δ_o. The indicator variable ι_y is set to 1 if the probability exceeds δ_o, and 0 otherwise (thus eliminating those classes as possibilities later in step 6). The second stage of the algorithm (steps 4–6) applies the binary SVMs from each class to the same input data, normalizes the resulting scores to two probability estimates per class (one for the match model and another for the non-match model), and then fuses and tests the probability estimates. Any fused probability exceeding the W-SVM rejection threshold δ_R indicates acceptance for a class. Note for brevity, only the process for classes '2' and '3' in steps 4 and 5 is shown (short circuit evaluation is possible using the indicator variables ι_0 and ι_1; an indicator variable with a value of 0 always results in a fused probability of 0). The bottom panel on the right shows where the data point for this example falls with respect to the CAP thresholded region (defined by the one-class SVM) and the overall W-SVM thresholded region for the class '3'.

Step 1. Apply One-class SVM CAP
Model for All Known Classes

Input: x = **Q**
$f_0^o(x) = s_0$ $f_1^o(x) = s_1$
$f_2^o(x) = s_2$ $f_3^o(x) = s_3$

Step 2. Normalize All One-class SVM Scores
Using EVT Models

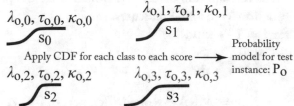

$\lambda_{0,0}, \tau_{0,0}, \kappa_{0,0}$ $\lambda_{0,1}, \tau_{0,1}, \kappa_{0,1}$
s_0 s_1

Apply CDF for each class to each score $\longrightarrow$

$\lambda_{0,2}, \tau_{0,2}, \kappa_{0,2}$ $\lambda_{0,3}, \tau_{0,3}, \kappa_{0,3}$
s_2 s_3

Probability
model for test
instance: P_O

Step 3. Test Probabilities

$P_o(0|x) < \delta_o, \iota_0 = 0$; $P_o(1|x) < \delta_o, \iota_1 = 0$;
$P_o(2|x) < \delta_o, \iota_2 = 0$; $P_o(3|x) < \delta_o, \iota_3 = 0$;

Step 4. Apply Indicator Variables to
Binary SVMs

$P_{\eta,0}(x) \times P_{\psi,0}(x) \times \iota_0 = 0 < \delta_R$
$P_{\eta,1}(x) \times P_{\psi,1}(x) \times \iota_1 = 0 < \delta_R$
$P_{\eta,2}(x) \times P_{\psi,2}(x) \times \iota_2 = 0.001 < \delta_R$
$P_{\eta,3}(x) \times P_{\psi,3}(x) \times \iota_3 = 0.877 > \delta_R$

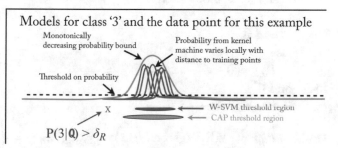

Models for class '3' and the data point for this example

Monotonically
decreasing probability bound

Probability from kernel
machine varies locally with
distance to training points

Threshold on probability

X

W-SVM threshold region
CAP threshold region

$P(3|\mathbf{Q}) > \delta_R$

Figure 5.6: **W-SVM testing when the input comes from an unknown class ('Q').** Classes marked in red indicate rejection. The procedure follows the same process depicted in Fig. 5.5. In this example, what happens when a data point falls outside the CAP thresholded region (i.e., exists in open space) for each known class is shown. The CAP models for the known classes do not produce probabilities that exceed the threshold δ_o, thus all of the indicator variables for the known classes ($\iota_0, \iota_1, \iota_2, \iota_3$) are set to 0, resulting in rejection for each class. The bottom panel on the right shows where the data point for this example falls with respect to the CAP thresholded region (defined by the one-class SVM) and the overall W-SVM thresholded region for the class '3'.

Algorithm 5.11 W-SVM multi-class probability estimation

Require:

    Classes y_i, $i = 1 \rightarrow k$;

    Pre-trained 1-vs-All binary SVM for each class y_i, with score function f_i;

    Pre-trained one-class SVM for each class y_i, with score functions f_i^o;

    Meta-Recognition object MR from libMR and parameter set $\mathcal{W}$.

    function W-SVM-Predict(test sample x)

1: **for** $i = 1 \rightarrow k$ **do**

2:   $\iota_i = 0$

3:   **if** $x > \tau_{o,i}$ **then**

4:     $P_{o,i} = \text{MR.W\_score}(f_i^o(x); \tau_{o,i}, \kappa_{o,i}, \lambda_{o,i}) = \left(1 - e^{-\left(\frac{-f_i^o(x) - \tau_{o,i}}{\lambda_{o,i}}\right)^{\kappa_{o,i}}}\right)$

5:     **if** $P_{o,i} > 0.001$ **then**

6:       $\iota_i = 1$;

7:     **end if**

8:   **else**

9:     $P_{o,i} = 0$

10:   **end if**

11:   **if** $x > \tau_{\eta,i}$ **then**

12:     $P_{\eta,i} = \text{MR.W\_score}(f_i(x); \tau_{\eta,i}, \kappa_{\eta,i}, \lambda_{\eta,i}) = \left(1 - e^{-\left(\frac{-f_i(x) - \tau_{\eta,i}}{\lambda_{\eta,i}}\right)^{\kappa_{\eta,i}}}\right)$

13:   **else**

14:     $P_{\eta,i} = 0$

15:   **end if**

16:   **if** $-x > \tau_{\psi,i}$ **then**

17:     $P_{\psi,i} = \text{MR.W\_score}(f_i(x); \tau_{\psi,i}, \kappa_{\psi,i}, \lambda_{\psi,i}) \left(e^{-\left(\frac{f_i(x) - \tau_{\psi,i}}{\lambda_{\psi,i}}\right)^{\kappa_{\psi,i}}}\right)$

18:   **else**

19:     $P_{\psi,i} = 0$

20:   **end if**

21: **end for**

22:

23: **return** $[P_{\eta,1}, P_{\psi,1}, \iota_1 \ldots, P_{\eta,k}, P_{\psi,k}, \iota_k]$ **end function**

Notice that twice as many models have been created during the training session, compared to what we observed for the P_I-SVM. This is because we require a one-class model and binary model per class. As we saw in Fig. 5.4, each of these models includes the parameters for the EVT models that were fit to them (one in the case of the one-class model, and two in the case of the binary model). A quick glance at the current directory will reveal that the training process also wrote two models to disk: `mnist.scale.3.model` and `mnist.scale.3.model_one_wsvm`. For a typical training run with libsvm, only one model file will be written.

Making predictions with the W-SVM requires a couple of additional parameters compared to what we needed for the P_I-SVM. Recall from the discussion of Eq. 5.7 that there are two probability thresholds δ_o and δ_R. In the example below, the one-class threshold δ_o corresponds to the -C flag and the binary threshold δ_R corresponds to the -P flag. In this example, we will vary the -P threshold, while keeping -C fixed to 0.001. This means we are looking for just a remote indication of association with a positive class via classification with the one-class model, before moving on to classification with the binary model. For the path to the model file, even though there are two model files on disk, we only need to specify the path to the `mnist.scale.3.model`.

```
$ ./svm-predict -P 0.0 -C 0.001 ./data/mnist.scale.t.openset
  mnist.scale.3.model outfile
Recognition Accuracy = 31.06%
Precision=0.311879, Recall=0.986972 Fmeasure=0.473981
Total tests=10000, True pos 3106 True Neg 0, False Pos 6853,
False neg 41

$ ./svm-predict -P 0.25 -C 0.001 ./data/mnist.scale.t.openset
  mnist.scale.3.model outfile
Recognition Accuracy = 66.69%
Precision=0.485401, Recall=0.972037 Fmeasure=0.647476
Total tests=10000, True pos 3059 True Neg 3610, False Pos 3243,
False neg 88

$ ./svm-predict -P 0.5 -C 0.001 ./data/mnist.scale.t.openset
  mnist.scale.3.model outfile
Recognition Accuracy = 82.9%
Precision=0.660846, Recall=0.938036 Fmeasure=0.775414
Total tests=10000, True pos 2952 True Neg 5338, False Pos 1515,
False neg 195

$ ./svm-predict -P 0.75 -C 0.001 ./data/mnist.scale.t.openset
  mnist.scale.3.model outfile
Recognition Accuracy = 82.51%
```

```
Precision=0.809019, Recall=0.581506 Fmeasure=0.676650
Total tests=10000, True pos 1830 True Neg 6421, False Pos 432,
False neg 1317


$ ./svm-predict -P 0.95 -C 0.001 ./data/mnist.scale.t.openset
  mnist.scale.3.model outfile
Recognition Accuracy = 74.65%
Precision=0.975155, Recall=0.199555 Fmeasure=0.331311
Total tests=10000, True pos 628 True Neg 6837, False Pos 16,
False neg 2519
```

The probability thresholds that we've iterated through above are the same ones we used to test the P_I-SVM in Sec. 5.3.1. With the flag -P 0.5, the W-SVM achieves an accuracy score of 82.9% compared to the P_I-SVM's score of 74.27% for the same threshold. In fact, none of the thresholds used in conjunction with the P_I-SVM lead to a result as good as this one. However, for the thresholds of 0.75 and 0.95, the accuracy for the W-SVM drops as the recall starts to get lower—these thresholds turn out to be too stringent. How one estimates the thresholds in practice is an open question. Experiments over training or validation data are helpful, but generalization to unseen data is not guaranteed. At the very least, calibration gives us an interpretable and consistent score space to threshold.

Scheirer et al. [2014a] evaluated the W-SVM over the same data sets considered by Jain et al. [2014]. For the open set partitions of MNIST and LETTER, as well as the Caltech 256 and ImageNet cross-data set test, the W-SVM proved to be superior in F-measure to the multi-attribute spaces algorithm, 1-vs-Rest multi-class SVM with a threshold, pairwise multi-class SVM with a threshold, and logistic regression with a threshold. If one compares the results from Scheirer et al. [2014a] and Jain et al. [2014], the W-SVM has a clear advantage in F-measure over the P_I-SVM. Given these results, is there any reason to use the P_I-SVM? If a smaller model is desired, or training time is more limited (depending on the underlying feature set), then the answer is yes. Further, only one threshold parameter needs to be set for testing when using the P_I-SVM.

Finally, the W-SVM is starting to gain traction in other fields of visual recognition beyond object recognition. In the realm of human biometrics, it was applied by Rattani et al. [2015] to the problem of fingerprint spoof detection, where an attacker attempts to fool a fingerprint recognition system by submitting known or unknown materials to a sensor. Because of the presence of unknown materials, this problem cannot be directly solved with off-the-shelf classifiers like SVM—it is, like the other problems we've discussed in this chapter, an open set recognition task. It was shown that the W-SVM demonstrated measurable improvement in classification accuracy for both novel material detection and spoof detection.

5.3.3   SPARSE REPRESENTATION-BASED OPEN SET RECOGNITION

An alternative to SVM, *sparse representation-based classification*, can also be considered in an EVT context. In its basic form, the algorithm is designed to choose the correct class during classification by searching for the sparsest representation of the input sample with respect to a training basis. When making a decision, the class reconstruction errors are used, making them attractive targets for EVT calibration. For open set recognition problems, Zhang and Patel [2017] suggest that most of the discriminative information for open set recognition is contained within the tails of the matched and sum of non-matched reconstruction error distributions, which can be modeled via the GPD. In this framing, open set recognition is then cast as a set of hypothesis matching problems.

Adapting a definition of open space risk from Scheirer et al. [2013], Zhang and Patel argue that the residuals r from the sparse code used for classification can also be used to model a proper measurable recognition function for open set recognition. The explanation given is that if an input sample corresponds to class k, then the reconstruction error associated with class k should be much lower than that of the other classes. Thus, it is likely that there is a distinction between matched and non-matched reconstruction errors. Taking this a step further, the reconstruction errors must follow some distribution. By fitting a probability model $P(r_k)$ to describe the distribution of the reconstruction errors of the matched class, the open set recognition problem can be reformulated as a hypothesis test for novelty detection:

$$\mathcal{H}_0 : P(r_k) \leq \delta$$
$$\mathcal{H}_1 : P(r_k) > \delta, \tag{5.8}$$

where the null hypothesis $\mathcal{H}_0$ implies that the test data are generated from the distribution $P(r_k)$, the alternative hypothesis $\mathcal{H}_1$ implies that the test data correspond to unknown classes, and $\delta \in [0, 1]$ is the threshold for rejection.

Because the underlying distribution of the data is unknown, it is not possible to create the model $P(r_k)$. Another option is to model the tail of the distribution, for which we have a good idea of what the distribution should be thanks to EVT. When considering the match distribution, only the right tail must be modeled. Zhang and Patel [2017] suggest the GPD distribution for this purpose, which yields the following hypothesis test:

$$\mathcal{H}_0 : G(r_k) \leq \delta_g$$
$$\mathcal{H}_1 : G(r_k) > \delta_g, \tag{5.9}$$

where $G(r_k)$ is the GPD distribution from the fit to the right tail of r_k, and δ_g is the rejection threshold.

As with many of the other algorithms we've examined in this book, non-match data is also available, this time in the form of non-matched reconstruction errors. Thus another hypothesis test, similar to Eq. 5.8, can be formulated using the left tail of the sum of all of the data across the non-matching classes. The two raw reconstruction errors (match and non-match) are then calibrated into probabilities by their corresponding GPD models. Similar to the probability of inclusion and exclusion strategy for the W-SVM, the two hypothesis testing problems here are combined to improve the accuracy of open set recognition. One key difference from the W-SVM algorithm is the use of a weighting factor that is multiplied against the calibrated non-match probability. That weight, w, is set as:

$$w = \frac{1}{3}(1 - \text{openness}), \tag{5.10}$$

where openness is the definition given by Scheirer et al. [2013] (Eq. 5.6).

Zhang and Patel [2017] examined the behavior of the resulting Sparse Representation-based Open Set classifier (SROSR) over several different visual recognition problems in the context of F-measure and accuracy. For face recognition, SROSR outperforms the W-SVM, Sparsity Concentration Index (SCI) (Wright et al. [2009]) and Ratio (Patel et al. [2012]) methods on the Yale-B data set (Belhumeur et al. [1997]), with very stable results across varying levels of problem openness (from 0%–40%). The same is true with respect to the MNIST data set of handwritten digits, but with steadily decreasing performance observed for all approaches as the problem grows to become more open (0%–14%). When considering the UIUC Attributes dataset (Farhadi et al. [2009]), even more rapidly decreasing performance is observed for all approaches as openness grows (2%–20%), even though SROSR maintains its advantage. Finally, for the Caltech 256 objects dataset, the largest gap in performance between SROSR and the comparison approaches is observed, with a good measure of stability for SROSR across multiple levels of problem openness (24%–30%).

5.3.4   EVT CALIBRATION FOR DEEP NETWORKS: OPENMAX

The very beginning of this book raised an important critique of visual recognition research in the period between 2012 and 2017: with so much emphasis placed on representation learning, little consideration has been given to decision making. The repercussions of this are felt every time a deep convolutional neural network is applied to a problem outside of the data set it was trained on—including scenarios with those pesky unknown samples we've been attempting to manage in this chapter. The two most common read-out layers used in deep learning are linear SVM and the Softmax function, which is a gradient-log-normalizer of the categorical probability distribution. Linear SVM is a bad choice for open set recognition problems (Scheirer et al. [2013]), but what about Softmax? Like linear SVM, it has no inherent ability to minimize the risk of the unknown. Moreover, Softmax leads to networks that are easily fooled by images that resemble noise with no semantic meaning (Nguyen et al. [2015]). To address this problem, Bendale and Boult [2016] recently introduced the OpenMax function, which is an EVT-calibrated decision function for deep convolutional neural networks.

The OpenMax function is predicated on the assumption that network values from the penultimate layer of the network (i.e., the Activation Vectors; see Fig. 5.7), are not an independent per-class score estimate, but instead a distribution of what classes are related. Algorithm 5.12 de-

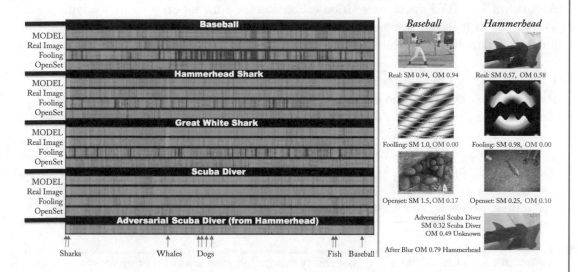

Figure 5.7: Deep convolutional neural networks are now ubiquitous for visual recognition tasks. But with a linear SVM or Softmax function as a read-out layer, they are not amenable to open set recognition. Bendale and Boult [2016] introduced a calibration method that uses elements of meta-recognition to support open set recognition. The OpenMax function is a replacement for Softmax that returns an estimate of an input being unknown to the recognition model. It works by measuring the distance between an activation vector for an input and the model vector for the top K classes, and calibrating the resulting distance scores via an EVT model to provide the final estimates. (Left) it can be seen that there is quite a bit of variation in the activation vectors from open set (i.e., out of class) and fooling (Nguyen et al. [2015]) images when compared to a real image or model from a class. (Right) The OpenMax function is able to make these distinctions, and assign more accurate probability scores to the various images than the Softmax function. From Bendale and Boult [2016].

scribes the calibration process, which is based on the meta-recognition algorithm we introduced in Chapter 3. Given a collection of classes and corresponding activation vectors, the mean μ_j of each collection of activation vectors for each class i is computed (line 2). The libMR FitHigh function is then used to fit a Weibull distribution over the largest distances between all correct positive training instances and the corresponding μ_j (line 3). Using the resulting model ρ_j (line 5), which contains the Weibull parameters, a rejection threshold can be applied over the probabilities calculated for a given input sample. Notice that this algorithm fits a Weibull distribution to the positive side of the decision boundary to model the probability of class inclusion—the same strategy used by the P_I-SVM.

The OpenMax function itself is computed via Alg. 5.13. It requires the means μ_j and EVT models ρ_j computed via Alg. 5.12 for all of the classes under consideration, along with

Algorithm 5.12 EVT meta-recognition calibration for open set deep networks, with per class Weibull fit to η largest distances to mean activation vector. Returns libMR models ρ_j, which includes parameters τ_i for shifting the data as well as the Weibull shape and scale parameters: κ_i, λ_i.

Require: FitHigh function from libMR
Require: Activation levels in the penultimate network layer $\mathbf{v}(\mathbf{x}) = v_1(x) \ldots v_N(x)$
Require: For each class j let $S_{i,j} = v_j(x_{i,j})$ for each correctly classified training example $x_{i,j}$.
1: **for** $j = 1 \ldots N$ **do**
2:    Compute mean activation vector, $\mu_j = \text{mean}_i(S_{i,j})$
3:    EVT fit $\rho_j = (\tau_j, \kappa_j, \lambda_j) = \text{FitHigh}(\|\hat{S}_j - \mu_j\|, \eta)$
4: **end for**
5: **return** means μ_j and libMR models ρ_j

Algorithm 5.13 OpenMax EVT probability estimation with rejection of unknown or uncertain inputs.

Require: Activation levels in the penultimate network layer $\mathbf{v}(\mathbf{x}) = v_1(x) \ldots v_N(x)$
Require: means μ_j and libMR models $\rho_j = (\tau_i, \lambda_i, \kappa_i)$
Require: α, the number of "top" classes to revise
1: Let $s(i) = \text{argsort}(v_j(x))$; Let $\omega_j = 1$
2: **for** $j = 1 \ldots \alpha$ **do**
3:    $\omega_{s(i)}(x) = 1 - \frac{\alpha-i}{\alpha} e^{-\left(\frac{\|x - \tau_{s(i)}\|}{\lambda_{s(i)}}\right)^{\kappa_{s(i)}}}$
4: **end for**
5: Revise activation vector $\hat{v}(x) = \mathbf{v}(\mathbf{x}) \circ \omega(\mathbf{x})$
6: Define $\hat{v}_0(x) = \sum_i v_i(x)(1 - \omega_i(x))$
7: $\hat{P}(y = j | \mathbf{x}) = \frac{e^{\hat{v}_j(x)}}{\sum_{i=0}^{N} e^{\hat{v}_i(x)}}$
8: Let $y^* = \text{argmax}_j P(y = j | \mathbf{x})$
9: Reject input if $y^* == 0$ or $P(y = y^* | \mathbf{x}) < \epsilon$

the activation vectors and the number α of top classes to revise via the probabilistic calibration. Because the OpenMax algorithm is tailored to open set recognition, it will assign an explicit class label ("0") to unknown inputs. The Weibull CDF probability (line 3) of the distance between $\mathbf{x}$ and μ_i is used as the basis of the rejection estimation. The probability scores are weighted as a function of α. Using the collection of weighted scores ω, a revised activation vector is computed (line 5), which changes the top scores. Following this, a pseudo-activation is computed for unknown class data, keeping the total activation constant (line 6). Including the pseudo-activation, the revised probabilities are calculated (line 7), and the maximum score is chosen as the predicted class (line 8). If the largest probability turned out to be for the unknown class, the input is rejected. The same is true if the probability doesn't exceed a pre-determined threshold ϵ.

Bendale and Boult [2016] performed a thorough evaluation to determine if OpenMax is better than Softmax on open set recognition problems. An advantage of the OpenMax approach is that it does not require re-training the underlying network architecture for feature extraction. Thus Bendale and Boult opted to use a pre-trained AlexNet model from the popular Caffe software package (Jia et al. [2014]). The data set considered in their experiments included all 1,000 categories from the ILSVRC 2012 validation set, fooling categories generated via the method of Nguyen et al. [2015] and previously unseen categories. The previously unseen categories are selected from ILSVRC 2010, which contains 360 classes that were not included in ILSVRC 2012. The complete test set contains 50,000 closed set images from ILSVRC 2012, 15,000 open set images (from the 360 different classes from ILSVRC 2010) and 15,000 fooling images (with 15 images each per ILSVRC 2012 category). The experiments showed that OpenMax consistently achieves higher F-measure scores than Softmax, giving us confidence in this much needed tool for open set decision making in deep learning.

CHAPTER 6

Summary and Future Directions

Each chapter in this book was a stepping stone toward a probabilistic framework for visual recognition using statistical extreme value theory. Starting with the foundation we laid in Chapters 1 and 2, we learned how EVT differs from central tendency modeling, which is the dominant mode of modeling in computer vision. With a general statistical paradigm that is well suited to modeling decision boundaries, which we hypothesize are defined by extrema, several different algorithmic strategies can be implemented that all rely on a distributional fit to some tail of a score distribution. The first strategy we looked at was meta-recognition, which was introduced in Chapter 3. Meta-Recognition is a general post-recognition score analysis technique for predicting failures in any type of recognition system that returns a distance or similarity score as its final decision. The recognition system could be anything from a simple application of Euclidean distance to a sophisticated supervised learning technique like a deep convolutional neural network with a Softmax layer for classification. In Chapter 4, the notion of meta-recognition was extended to score normalization. Instead of just making a prediction of success or failure, an EVT-based normalization makes use of the CDF of an EVT distribution to produce a probability score reflecting the confidence of class membership. A normalized probability score is a more interpretable output that is useful when combining decisions or classifiers. And finally, in Chapter 5, score normalization was applied directly to supervised machine learning classifiers to calibrate their output. Various strategies were introduced for this, including one-sided and two-sided EVT fitting procedures, to achieve good probability estimates even in the face of unknown inputs coming into the classifier.

What is the next logical step beyond the *post hoc* calibration in an algorithm like the W-SVM or convolutional neural network with OpenMax? If an EVT fitting process is inherent in the learning objective of the training procedure for a classifier, it may be possible to define the decision boundary itself from extrema points identified within the training data. We are already starting to see implementations of this idea emerging as an alternative to kernel machines. The Extreme Value Machine of Rudd et al. [2015] has a well-grounded interpretation derived from EVT, and is the first classifier of its kind to be able to perform nonlinear, kernel-free, variable bandwidth, incremental learning. In an incremental learning regime, unknown inputs in an open set recognition problem can be identified, given an arbitrary label, and inserted into an existing classifier as a new class to be recognized. The EVM is a good solution to this problem, in that it is far more scalable than a Nearest Neighbor, RBF SVM or W-SVM classifier for such model updates.

The extension to incremental learning is just one potential direction within the rather broad problem of open set recognition. Much more is possible with respect to modeling the fundamentals of sensory perception. Analysis by synthesis is a classic idea within computer vision that is seeing a resurgence (Kulkarni et al. [2015], Yildirim et al. [2015]). In essence, the recognition process eschews the usual tactic of attempting to match a 2D input image to a learned model capturing the variance of a training data set in favor of the synthesis of a set of parameters from a learned model that explains the 2D input. Generative models facilitating one-shot learning are an important goal of research in this area. To date, there has been no work on generative models for visual recognition underpinned by EVT—this is an intriguing possibility. The choice of an underlying distribution to sample from is often an afterthought, and inevitably leads back to a Gaussian model of some form. Perhaps sampling at the extremes will lead to decision models with better generalizability, as was suggested in Chapter 1 of this book.

In a closed set context, one can draw connections between EVT modeling and decision theory (Berger [2013], Chernoff and Moses [1986]), which is concerned with modeling the choices made by an individual agent. For instance, a visual recognition model is an individual agent that makes decisions over images submitted as input. It is common to apply statistical distributions to define the utility functions, regret functions, and models of states and actions that exist within the sphere of decision theory. There is good potential for EVT to fit into existing decision frameworks—especially in cases where extrema that have a strong impact on decision making are treated as events too rare to consider by the model. However, in an open set context, decision theory does not apply, as truly unknown inputs fall outside the purvey of the model. Research into addressing this deficit, perhaps with EVT, is necessary if decision theory is to be applied to many real-world problems in visual recognition.

Before closing this volume, a few words should be said about the limitations of EVT-based modeling. There are two important considerations that must be made before turning to EVT when designing an algorithm for visual recognition. First, one must ask what, if any, extrema are present for the given problem at hand. Determining what data are extrema is not a straightforward task. The algorithms introduced in this book have largely relied upon approximate identification (e.g., tail modeling), followed by an empirical evaluation of the resulting model. This reduces the problem to one of choosing a free parameter for the statistical estimation, but it doesn't answer the fundamental question of what extrema are present. If one chooses too many points that are not extrema, or not enough points that are, an inaccurate model will result. Second, if more than one dimension is available per data point, there is presently no good way to perform a statistical fit using the distributions that have been introduced in this book. The current solution to this problem is an aggressive quantization or compression that reduces the dimensionality down to a single dimension. This procedure is not ideal if information is being lost in the process. Even taken together, these two limitations are not necessary show-stopping problems, and should be thought of as areas of improvement that can be addressed by further research.

Coming full circle from where we started in Chapter 1, the brain represents the frontier of both natural science and computer science. An understanding of neural computation will inevitably lead to more powerful machine learning algorithms. While symmetric Gaussian-like tuning curves are prevalent in the brain, they are by no means the rule. Indeed, even cells with classically Gaussian-like tuning curves in one stimulus dimension—such as local orientation in V1 simple cells—frequently have asymmetric, extrema-oriented tuning along another axis, such as contrast. Such mixed models may be better modeled with EVT-based distributions that easily include both symmetric and asymmetric aspects. Based on the results from wet-bench research examining the above cellular-level phenomena, Banerjee et al. [2016] are creating computational neural models that leverage the principles of EVT to simulate and predict the consequence of sensory integration in retinal function in the zebrafish. The overall objective of that work is to uncover facets of the mathematical and algorithmic underpinnings of sensory integration in the brain, with the dual goal of advancing understanding in biology and building more robust and powerful artificial information processing systems. Work along these lines will no doubt accelerate in the coming years as the intersection between neuroscience and machine learning grows.

Bibliography

F. G. Ashby and L. A. Alfonso-Reese. Categorization as probability density estimation. *Journal of Mathematical Psychology*, 39 (2): 216–233, 1995. DOI: 10.1006/jmps.1995.1021. 2, 6

F. G. Ashby and W. T. Maddox. Relations between prototype, exemplar, and decision bound models of categorization. *Journal of Mathematical Psychology*, 37 (3): 372–400, 1993. DOI: 10.1006/jmps.1993.1023. 4, 8

F. G. Ashby and W. T. Maddox. Human category learning. *Annu. Rev. Psychol*, 56: 149–178, 2005. DOI: 10.1146/annurev.psych.56.091103.070217. 4

F. G. Ashby and N. A Perrin. Toward a unified theory of similarity and recognition. *Psychological Review*, 95 (1): 124, 1988. DOI: 10.1037//0033-295x.95.1.124. 8

S. Banerjee, W. J. Scheirer, and L. Li. Cross-modal sensory information integration in modulation of vertebrate visual system functions. Program 244.01, Neuroscience Meeting Planner, 2016. http://www.abstractsonline.com/pp8/index.html#!/4071/presentation/13150 97

A. Bansal, A. Farhadi, and D. Parikh. Towards transparent systems: Semantic characterization of failure modes. In *European Conference on Computer Vision (ECCV)*, pages 366–381. Springer, 2014. DOI: 10.1007/978-3-319-10599-4_24. 31

M. Bao, L. Yang, C. Rios, B. He, and S. A. Engel. Perceptual learning increases the strength of the earliest signals in visual cortex. *The Journal of Neuroscience*, 30 (45): 15080–15084, 2010. DOI: 10.1523/jneurosci.5703-09.2010. 6

E. Barenholtz and M. Tarr. Visual judgment of similarity across shape transformations: Evidence for a compositional model of articulated objects. *Acta Psychologica*, 128: 331–338, May 2008. DOI: 10.1016/j.actpsy.2008.03.007. 5

J. C. Bartlett, S. Hurry, and W. Thorley. Typicality and familiarity of faces. *Memory and Cognition*, 12 (3): 219–228, May 1984. DOI: 10.3758/bf03197669. 5

M. S. Bartlett and J. Tanaka. An attractor field model of face representation: Effects of typicality and image morphing. In *Psychonomics Society Satellite Symposium on Object Perception and Memory (OPAM)*, 1998. 5

P. L. Bartlett and A. Tewari. Sparseness vs. estimating conditional probabilities: Some asymptotic results. *Journal of Machine Learning Research*, 8 (4): 775–790, 2007. DOI: 10.1007/978-3-540-27819-1_39. 73

P. N. Belhumeur, J. P. Hespanha, and D. J. Kriegman. Eigenfaces vs. fisherfaces: Recognition using class specific linear projection. *IEEE Transactions on Pattern Analysis and Machine Intelligence*, 19 (7): 711–720, 1997. DOI: 10.1109/34.598228. 90

A. Bendale and T. E. Boult. Towards open set deep networks. In *IEEE Conference on Computer Vision and Pattern Recognition (CVPR)*, June 2016. DOI: 10.1109/cvpr.2016.173. 90, 91, 93

Y. Bengio. Learning deep architectures for AI. *Foundational and Trends in Machine Learning*, 2 (1), 2009. DOI: 10.1561/2200000006. 1

Y. Bensalah. *Steps in Applying Extreme Value Theory to Finance: A Review*. Bank of Canada, 2000. 35

J. O. Berger. *Statistical Decision Theory and Bayesian Analysis*. Springer Science and Business Media, 2013. DOI: 10.1007/978-1-4757-4286-2. 96

P. Berkes, G. Orbán, M. Lengyel, and J. Fiser. Spontaneous cortical activity reveals hallmarks of an optimal internal model of the environment. *Science*, 331 (6013): 83–87, 2011. DOI: 10.1126/science.1195870. 1

S. M. Berman. Limiting distribution of the maximum term in sequences of dependent random variables. *The Annals of Mathematical Statistics*, 33 (3): 894–908, 1962. DOI: 10.1214/aoms/1177704458. 7, 28

E. Bertin and M. Clusel. Generalized extreme value statistics and sum of correlated variables. *Journal of Physics A: Mathematical General*, 39: 7607–7619, June 2006. DOI: 10.1088/0305-4470/39/24/001. 7

J. R. Beveridge. Face recognition vendor test 2006 experiment 4 covariate study, 2008. Presentation at 1st MBGC Kick-off Workshop. 30

J. R. Beveridge, G. Givens, P. J. Phillips, and B. Draper. Focus on quality, predicting FRVT 2006 performance. In *Intl. Conf. on Automatic Face and Gesture Recognition*, 2008. DOI: 10.1109/afgr.2008.4813375. 30

A. S. Brahmachari and S. Sarkar. BLOGS: Balanced local and global search for non-degenerate two view epipolar geometry. In *International Conference on Computer Vision (ICCV)*, 2009. DOI: 10.1109/iccv.2009.5459379. 59

J. B. Broadwater and R. Chellappa. Adaptive threshold estimation via extreme value theory. *IEEE Transactions on Signal Processing*, 58 (2): 490–500, 2010. DOI: 10.1109/tsp.2009.2031285. 19, 26, 65

G. Burghouts, A. Smeulders, and J.-M. Geusebroek. The distribution family of similarity distances. In *Advances in Neural Information Processing Systems (NIPS)*, 2008. 60

E. Castillo. *Extreme Value Theory in Engineering*. Academic Press, 1988. 17

V. Chandola, A. Banerjee, and V. Kumar. Anomaly detection: A survey. *ACM Computing Surveys (CSUR)*, 41 (3): 15, 2009. DOI: 10.1145/1541880.1541882. 7

C.-C. Chang and C.-J. Lin. LIBSVM: A library for support vector machines. *ACM Transactions on Intelligent Systems and Technology*, 2: 27:1–27:27, 2011. Software available at http://www.csie.ntu.edu.tw/~cjlin/libsvm. DOI: 10.1145/1961189.1961199. 75

H. Chernoff and L. E. Moses. *Elementary Decision Theory*. Dover Publications, 1986. 96

C. Chow. On optimum recognition error and reject tradeoff. *IEEE Transactions on Information Theory*, 16 (1): 41–46, 1970. DOI: 10.1109/tit.1970.1054406. 75

O. Chum and J. Matas. Matching with prosac-progressive sample consensus. In *IEEE Conference on Computer Vision and Pattern Recognition (CVPR)*, 2005. DOI: 10.1109/cvpr.2005.221. 59

O. Chum, J. Matas, and J. Kittler. Locally optimized RANSAC. In *Joint Pattern Recognition Symposium*, pages 236–243. Springer, 2003. DOI: 10.1007/978-3-540-45243-0_31. 56

S. Coles. *An Introduction to Statistical Modeling of Extreme Values*. Springer, 2001. DOI: 10.1007/978-1-4471-3675-0. 13

R. M. Colwill and R. A. Rescorla. Associations between the discriminative stimulus and the reinforcer in instrumental learning. *Journal of Experimental Psychology: Animal Behavior Processes*, 14 (2): 155, 1988. DOI: 10.1037//0097-7403.14.2.155. 6

D. D. Cox. Do we understand high-level vision? *Current Opinion in Neurobiology*, 25: 187–193, 2014. DOI: 10.1016/j.conb.2014.01.016. 1

M. Cox. Metacognition in computation: A selected research review. *Artificial Intelligence*, 169 (2): 104–141, 2005. DOI: 10.1016/j.artint.2005.10.009. 32

S. Daftry, S. Zeng, J. A. Bagnell, and M. Hebert. Introspective perception: Learning to predict failures in vision systems. In *IEEE/RSJ International Conference on Intelligent Robots and Systems (IROS)*, 2016. DOI: 10.1109/iros.2016.7759279. 31

D. Danks. Theory unification and graphical models in human categorization. *Causal Learning: Psychology, Philosophy, and Computation*, pages 173–189, 2007. DOI: 10.1093/acprof:oso/9780195176803.003.0012. 2

R. Datta, D. Joshi, J. Li, and J. Z. Wang. Image retrieval: Ideas, influences, and trends of the new age. *ACM Computing Surveys (CSUR)*, 40 (2): 5, 2008. DOI: 10.1145/1348246.1348248. 55

L. de Haan and A. Ferreira. *Extreme Value Theory: An Introduction.* Springer Science and Business Media, 2007. DOI: 10.1007/0-387-34471-3. 13, 26, 37

N. Debbabi, M. Kratz, M. Mboup, and S. El Asmi. Combining algebraic approach with extreme value theory for spike detection. In *20th European Signal Processing Conference (EUSIPCO)*, pages 1836–1840, 2012. 6

J. DeWinter and J. Wagemans. Perceptual saliency of points along the contour of everyday objects: A large-scale study. *Perception and Psychophysics*, 70 (1): 50–64, January 2008. DOI: 10.3758/pp.70.1.50. 5

J. J. DiCarlo and D. D. Cox. Untangling invariant object recognition. *Trends in Cognitive Sciences*, 11: 333–341, 2007. DOI: 10.1016/j.tics.2007.06.010. 1

W. Einhäuser, M. Spain, and P. Perona. Objects predict fixations better than early saliency. *Journal of Vision*, 8 (14): 1–26, November 2008. DOI: 10.1167/8.14.18. 5

N. Eshel, J. Tian, and N. Uchida. Opening the black box: Dopamine, predictions, and learning. *Trends in Cognitive Sciences*, 17 (9): 430–431, 2013. DOI: 10.1016/j.tics.2013.06.010. 31

W. K. Estes. Discriminative conditioning. I. A discriminative property of conditioned anticipation. *Journal of Experimental Psychology*, 32 (2): 150, 1943. DOI: 10.1037/h0058316. 6

Ali Farhadi, Ian Endres, Derek Hoiem, and David Forsyth. Describing objects by their attributes. In *Computer Vision and Pattern Recognition, (CVPR). IEEE Conference on*, pages 1778–1785, 2009. DOI: 10.1109/cvprw.2009.5206772. 90

R. Fergus. Deep learning for computer vision, 2013. http://cs.nyu.edu/~fergus/presentations/nips2013_final.pdf Tutorial Presented at NIPS 2013. 67

B. Fernando, S. Karaoglu, and A. Trémeau. Extreme value theory based text binarization in documents and natural scenes. *International Conference on Machine Vision (ICMV)*, pages 144–151, 2010. 60

M. A. Fischler and R. C. Bolles. Random sample consensus: A paradigm for model fitting with applications to image analysis and automated cartography. *Communications of the ACM*, 24 (6): 381–395, 1981. DOI: 10.1145/358669.358692. 56

R. A. Fisher and L. H. C. Tippett. Limiting forms of the frequency distribution of the largest or smallest member of a sample. *Mathematical Proceedings of the Cambridge Philosophical Society*, 24 (02): 180–190, 1928. DOI: 10.1017/s0305004100015681. 17

J. H. Flavell and H. M. Wellman. Metamemory. In R. V. Kail Jr. and J. W. Hagen, Eds., *Perspectives on the Development of Memory and Cognition*, pages 3–33. LEA, 1988. 31

P. Flynn. ICE mining: Quality and demographic investigations of ice 2006 performance results, 2008. Presentation at 1st MBGC Workshop. DOI: 10.1007/978-1-4471-4402-1_5. 30

V. Fragoso and M. Turk. SWIGS: A swift guided sampling method. In *IEEE Conference on Computer Vision and Pattern Recognition (CVPR)*, June 2013. DOI: 10.1109/cvpr.2013.357. 2, 8, 19, 24, 26, 41, 58

V. Fragoso, P. Sen, S. Rodriguez, and M. Turk. EVSAC: Accelerating hypotheses generation by modeling matching scores with extreme value theory. In *IEEE International Conference on Computer Vision (ICCV)*, December 2013. DOI: 10.1109/iccv.2013.307. 2, 8, 42, 56, 57, 59

W. Freiwald, D.Y. Tsao, and M.S. Livingstone. A face feature space in the macaque temporal lobe. *Nature Neuroscience*, 12 (9): 1187–1198, September 2009. DOI: 10.1038/nn.2363. 2, 5, 6

G. Fumera and F. Roli. Support vector machines with embedded reject option. In *Pattern Recognition with Support Vector Machines*, pages 68–82. Springer, 2002. DOI: 10.1007/3-540-45665-1_6. 72

C. S. Furmanski and S. A. Engel. An oblique effect in human primary visual cortex. *Nature Neuroscience*, 3: 535–536, 2000. DOI: 10.1038/75702. 6

T. Furon and H. Jégou. Using extreme value theory for image detection. Technical Report RR-8244, INRIA, 2013. 19, 26, 62

X. Gibert, V. Patel, and R. Chellappa. Sequential score adaptation with extreme value theory for robust railway track inspection. In *Proc. of the IEEE International Conference on Computer Vision Workshops*, 2015a. DOI: 10.1109/iccvw.2015.27. 19, 26, 64

X. Gibert, V. M. Patel, and R. Chellappa. Robust fastener detection for autonomous visual railway track inspection. In *IEEE Winter Conference on Applications of Computer Vision (WACV)*, 2015b. DOI: 10.1109/wacv.2015.98. 66

M. Going and J. D. Read. Effects of uniqueness, sex of subject, and sex of photograph on facial recognition. *Perceptual and Motor Skills*, 39: 109–110, August 1974. DOI: 10.2466/pms.1974.39.1.109. 5

L. Goshen and I. Shimshoni. Balanced exploration and exploitation model search for efficient epipolar geometry estimation. *IEEE Transactions on Pattern Analysis and Machine Intelligence*, 30 (7): 1230–1242, 2008. DOI: 10.1109/tpami.2007.70768. 59

T. L. Griffiths, K. R. Canini, A. N. Sanborn, and D. J. Navarro. Unifying rational models of categorization via the hierarchical Dirichlet process. In *Proc. of the 29th Annual Conference of the Cognitive Science Society*, pages 323–328, 2007. 2, 4

T. L. Griffiths, A. N. Sanborn, K. R. Canini, D. J. Navarro, and J. B. Tenenbaum. Nonparametric Bayesian models of categorization. In E. M. Pothos and A. J. Wills, Eds., *Formal Approaches in Categorization*, chapter 8, pages 173–198. Cambridge University Press, 2011. DOI: 10.1017/cbo9780511921322. 2

I. I. A. Groen, S. Ghebreab, V. A. F. Lamme, and H. S. Scholte. Spatially pooled contrast responses predict neural and perceptual similarity of naturalistic image categories. *PLOS Computational Biology*, 8 (10): e1002726, 2012. DOI: 10.1371/journal.pcbi.1002726. 2, 6

P. Grother and E. Tabassi. Performance of biometric quality evaluations. *IEEE Transactions on Pattern Analysis and Machine Intelligence*, 29 (4): 531–543, 2007. DOI: 10.1109/tpami.2007.1019. 29

E. J. Gumbel. *Statistical Theory of Extreme Values and Some Practical Applications*. Number National Bureau of Standards Applied Mathematics in 33. U.S. GPO, Washington, DC, 1954. DOI: 10.1017/s0368393100099958. 7, 13

F. R. Hampel, E. M. Ronchetti, P. J. Rousseeuw, and W. A. Stahel. *Robust Statistics: The Approach Based on Influence Functions*. John Wiley & Sons, 2011. DOI: 10.1002/9781118186435. 47

M. N. Hebart, T. H. Donner, and J. D. Haynes. Human visual and parietal cortex encode visual choices independent of motor plans. *NeuroImage*, 2012. DOI: 10.1016/j.neuroimage.2012.08.027. 6

ImagetNet Large Scale Visual Recognition Challenge 2012 (ILSVRC2012). `http://image-net.org/challenges/lsvrc/2012/index`, Accessed: 2016-08-20. 9

ImagetNet Large Scale Visual Recognition Challenge 2015 (ILSVRC2015). `http://image-net.org/challenges/lsvrc/2015/index`, Accessed: 2016-08-20. 70

L. Itti and C. Koch. Computational modeling of visual attention. *Nature Reviews Neuroscience*, 2 (3): 194–203, February 2001. 5

A. Jain, K. Nandakumar, and A. Ross. Score normalization in multimodal biometric systems. *Pattern Recognition*, 38 (12): 2270–2285, 2005. DOI: 10.1016/j.patcog.2005.01.012. 46

L. P. Jain, W. J. Scheirer, and T. E. Boult. Multi-class open set recognition using probability of inclusion. In *European Conference on Computer Vision (ECCV)*, September 2014. DOI: 10.1007/978-3-319-10578-9_26. 8, 26, 70, 72, 73, 78, 88

H. Jégou, M. Douze, and C. Schmid. Hamming embedding and weak geometric consistency for large scale image search. In *European Conference on Computer Vision (ECCV)*. Springer, 2008. DOI: 10.1007/978-3-540-88682-2_24. 55

H. Jégou, M. Douze, and C. Schmid. Improving bag-of-features for large scale image search. *International Journal of Computer Vision*, 87 (3): 316–336, 2010. DOI: 10.1007/s11263-009-0285-2. 63

A. Jern and C. Kemp. A probabilistic account of exemplar and category generation. *Cognitive Psychology*, 66 (1): 85–125, 2013. DOI: 10.1016/j.cogpsych.2012.09.003. 1, 3, 6

Yangqing Jia, Evan Shelhamer, Jeff Donahue, Sergey Karayev, Jonathan Long, Ross Girshick, Sergio Guadarrama, and Trevor Darrell. Caffe: Convolutional architecture for fast feature embedding. *arXiv Preprint arXiv:1408.5093*, 2014. DOI: 10.1145/2647868.2654889. 93

J. Kantner and J. Tanaka. Experience produces the atypicality bias in object perception. *Perception*, 41: 556–568, June 2012. DOI: 10.1068/p7096. 5

S. Kotz and S. Nadarajah. *Extreme Value Distributions: Theory and Applications*. World Scientific Publishing Co., 1st ed., 2001. DOI: 10.1142/9781860944024. 2, 17, 49

A. Krizhevsky and G. E. Hinton. Learning multiple layers of features from tiny images. Technical report, University of Toronto, 2009. 61

A. Krizhevsky, I. Sutskever, and G. E. Hinton. Imagenet classification with deep convolutional neural networks. In *Advances in Neural Information Processing Systems (NIPS)*, 2012. 9

J. K. Kruschke. ALCOVE: An exemplar-based connectionist model of category learning. *Psychological Review*, 99 (1): 22, 1992. DOI: 10.1037//0033-295x.99.1.22. 4

J. K. Kruschke. Models of attentional learning. In E. M. Pothos and A. J. Wills, Eds., *Formal Approaches in Categorization*, chapter 6, pages 120–152. Cambridge University Press, 2011. DOI: 10.1017/cbo9780511921322. 6

T. D. Kulkarni, P. Kohli, J. B. Tenenbaum, and V. Mansinghka. Picture: A probabilistic programming language for scene perception. In *IEEE Conference on Computer Vision and Pattern Recognition (CVPR)*, 2015. DOI: 10.1109/cvpr.2015.7299068. 96

N. Kumar, A. C. Berg, P. N. Belhumeur, and S. Nayar. Describable visual attributes for face verification and image search. *IEEE Transactions on Pattern Analysis and Machine Intelligence*, 33 (10): 1962–1977, 2011. DOI: 10.1109/tpami.2011.48. 69, 70

J. T.-Y. Kwok. Moderating the outputs of support vector machine classifiers. *IEEE Transactions on Neural Networks*, 10 (5): 1018–1031, 1999. DOI: 10.1109/72.788642. 72

J. A. Lasserre, C. M. Bishop, and T. P. Minka. Principled hybrids of generative and discriminative models. In *IEEE Conference on Computer Vision and Pattern Recognition (CVPR)*, 2006. DOI: 10.1109/cvpr.2006.227. 72

Y. LeCun, L. Bottou, Y. Bengio, and P. Haffner. Gradient-based learning applied to document recognition. *Proc. of the IEEE*, 86 (11): 2278–2324, 1998. DOI: 10.1109/5.726791. 71, 72, 76

Y. LeCun, Y. Bengio, and G. E. Hinton. Deep learning. *Nature*, 521: 436–444, 2015. DOI: 10.1038/nature14539. 1, 9

K. Lee, G. Byatt, and G. Rhodes. Caricature effects, distinctiveness, and identification: Testing the face-space framework. *Psychological Science*, 11 (5): 379–385, September 2000. DOI: 10.1111/1467-9280.00274. 5

D. Leopold, A. J. O'Toole, T. Vetter, and V. Blanz. Prototype-referenced shape encoding revealed by high-level after effects. *Nature Neuroscience*, 4 (1): 89–94, January 2001. DOI: 10.1038/82947. 2, 5

D. Leopold, G. Rhodes, K. Müller, and L. Jeffery. The dynamics of visual adaptation to faces. *Proc. of the Royal Society B*, 272: 897–904, May 2005. DOI: 10.1098/rspb.2004.3022. 5

D. Leopold, I. Bondar, and M. Giese. Norm-based face encoding by single neurons in the monkey inferotemporal cortex. *Nature*, 442: 572–575, August 2006. DOI: 10.1038/nature04951. 2, 4, 5

M. B. Lewis and R. A. Johnston. Understanding caricatures of faces. *The Quarterly Journal of Experimental Psychology Section A: Human Experimental Psychology*, 51 (2): 321–346, May 1998. DOI: 10.1080/713755758. 5

W. Li, X. Gao, and T. E. Boult. Predicting biometric system failure. In *IEEE International Conference on Computational Intelligence for Homeland Security and Personal Safety*, 2005. DOI: 10.1109/cihsps.2005.1500612. 30

Z. Li, O. Vinyals, H. Baker, and R. Bajcsy. Feature learning using generalized extreme value distribution based K-means clustering. In *International Conference on Pattern Recognition (ICPR)*, 2012. 19, 24, 60

S. Lloyd. Least squares quantization in PCM. *IEEE Transactions on Information Theory*, 28 (2): 129–137, 1982. DOI: 10.1109/tit.1982.1056489. 60

F. M. Longin. From value at risk to stress testing: The extreme value approach. *Journal of Banking and Finance*, 24 (7): 1097–1130, 2000. DOI: 10.1016/s0378-4266(99)00077-1. 17

B. C. Love, D. L. Medin, and T. M. Gureckis. SUSTAIN: A network model of category learning. *Psychological review*, 111 (2): 309, 2004. DOI: 10.1037/0033-295x.111.2.309. 4

D. G. Lowe. Distinctive image features from scale-invariant keypoints. *International Journal of Computer Vision*, 60 (2): 91–110, 2004. DOI: 10.1023/b:visi.0000029664.99615.94. 58

C. J. Maddison, D. Tarlow, and T. Minka. A* sampling. In *Advances in Neural Information Processing Systems (NIPS)*, 2014. 19

T. Malisiewicz, A. Gupta, and A. A. Efros. Ensemble of exemplar-SVMs for object detection and beyond. In *International Conference on Computer Vision (ICCV)*, 2011. DOI: 10.1109/iccv.2011.6126229. 72

A. Martin, G. Doddington, T. Kamm, M. Ordowski, and M. Przybocki. The DET curve in assessment of detection task performance. In *5th European Conference on Speech Communication and Technology*, 1997. 39

R. Mauro and M. Kubovy. Caricature and face recognition. *Memory and Cognition*, 20 (4): 433–440, July 1992. DOI: 10.3758/bf03210927. 5

K. McAlonan, J. Cavanaugh, and R. H. Wurtz. Guarding the gateway to cortex with attention in visual thalamus. *Nature*, 456 (7220): 391–394, 2008. DOI: 10.1038/nature07382. 6

D. Michie, D. J. Spiegelhalter, C. C. Taylor, and J. Campbell, Eds. *Machine Learning, Neural and Statistical Classification*. Ellis Horwood, 1994. 79

J. P. Minda and J. D. Smith. Prototype models of categorization: Basic formulation, predictions, and limitations. In E. M. Pothos and A. J. Wills, Eds., *Formal Approaches in Categorization*, chapter 3, pages 40–64. Cambridge University Press, 2011. DOI: 10.1017/cbo9780511921322. 4

National Institute of Standards and Technology. NIST biometric scores set, 2004. http://www.itl.nist.gov/iad/894.03/biometricscores/ 37, 40, 41, 54, 55

National Institute of Standards and Technology. *NIST/SEMATECH e-Handbook of Statistical Methods*. 33. U.S. GPO, 2012. 7, 13, 35, 56

A. Nguyen, J. Yosinski, and J. Clune. Deep neural networks are easily fooled: High confidence predictions for unrecognizable images. In *IEEE Conference on Computer Vision and Pattern Recognition (CVPR)*, June 2015. DOI: 10.1109/cvpr.2015.7298640. 9, 90, 91, 93

D. Nister and H. Stewenius. Scalable recognition with a vocabulary tree. In *IEEE Conference on Computer Vision and Pattern Recognition (CVPR)*, 2006. DOI: 10.1109/cvpr.2006.264. 63

R. M. Nosofsky. Tests of an exemplar model for relating perceptual classification and recognition memory. *Journal of Experimental Psychology: Human Perception and Performance*, 17 (1): 3, 1991. DOI: 10.1037//0096-1523.17.1.3. 4

R. M. Nosofsky. The generalized context model: An exemplar model of classification. In E. M. Pothos and A. J. Wills, Eds., *Formal Approaches in Categorization*, chapter 2, pages 18–39. Cambridge University Press, 2011. ISBN 9780521190480. DOI: 10.1017/cbo9780511921322. 4, 8

R. M. Nosofsky and D. R. Little. Classification response times in probabilistic rule-based category structures: Contrasting exemplar-retrieval and decision-boundary models. *Memory and Cognition*, 38 (7): 916–927, 2010. DOI: 10.3758/mc.38.7.916. 8

R. M. Nosofsky, M. A. Gluck, T. J. Palmeri, S. C. McKinley, and P. Glauthier. Comparing modes of rule-based classification learning: A replication and extension of Shepard, Hovland, and Jenkins (1961). *Memory and Cognition*, 22 (3): 352–369, 1994a. DOI: 10.3758/bf03200862. 4

R. M. Nosofsky, T. J. Palmeri, and S. C. McKinley. Rule-plus-exception model of classification learning. *Psychological Review; Psychological Review*, 101 (1): 53, 1994b. DOI: 10.1037//0033-295x.101.1.53. 4

K. Okada, J. Steffans, T. Maurer, H. Hong, E. Elagin, H. Neven, and C. Malsburg. The Bochum/USC face recognition system and how it fared in the FERET phase III test. In H. Wechsler, P. J. Phillips, V. Bruce, F. Fogeman Soulie, and T. S. Huang, Eds., *Face Recognition: From Theory to Applications*, pages 186–205. Springer-Verlag, 1998. DOI: 10.1007/978-3-642-72201-1. 40, 41

B. A. Olshausen and D. J. Field. Emergence of simple-cell receptive field properties by learning a sparse code for natural images. *Nature*, 381, June 1996. DOI: 10.1038/381607a0. 1

B. A. Olshausen and D. J. Field. Sparse coding of sensory inputs. *Current Opinion in Neurobiology*, 14 (4): 481–487, 2004. DOI: 10.1016/j.conb.2004.07.007. 1

V. M. Patel, T. Wu, S. Biswas, P. J. Phillips, and R. Chellappa. Dictionary-based face recognition under variable lighting and pose. *IEEE Transactions on Information Forensics and Security*, 7 (3): 954–965, 2012. DOI: 10.1109/tifs.2012.2189205. 90

F. Perronnin, Y. Liu, and J.-M. Renders. A family of contextual measures of similarity between distributions with application to image retrieval. In *IEEE Conference on Computer Vision and Pattern Recognition (CVPR)*, 2009. DOI: 10.1109/cvprw.2009.5206505. 63

M. Peterson and G. Rhodes. *Perception of Faces, Objects and Scenes: Analytic and Holistic Processes*. Oxford University Press, 2003. DOI: 10.1093/acprof:oso/9780195313659.001.0001. 5

J. Philbin, O. Chum, M. Isard, J. Sivic, and A. Zisserman. Object retrieval with large vocabularies and fast spatial matching. In *IEEE Conference on Computer Vision and Pattern Recognition (CVPR)*, 2007. DOI: 10.1109/cvpr.2007.383172. 63

P. J. Phillips and J. R. Beveridge. An introduction to biometric-completeness: The equivalence of matching and quality. In *IEEE International Conference on Biometrics: Theory, Applications, and Systems (BTAS)*, 2009. DOI: 10.1109/btas.2009.5339055. 30

J. Pickands. Statistical inference using extreme order statistics. *The Annals of Statistics*, pages 119–131, 1975. DOI: 10.1214/aos/1176343003. 18

J. Platt. Probabilistic outputs for support vector machines and comparison to regularized likelihood methods. In A. Smola, P. Bartlett, and B. Schölkopf, Eds., *Advances in Large Margin Classifiers*. MIT Press, 2000. 72, 73

E. M. Pothos and T. M. Bailey. Predicting category intuitiveness with the rational model, the simplicity model, and the generalized context model. *Journal of Experimental Psychology: Learning, Memory, and Cognition*, 35 (4): 1062, 2009. DOI: 10.1037/a0015903. 6

R. F. Quick. A vector-magnitude model of contrast detection. *Biological Cybernetics*, 16 (2): 65–67, 1974. DOI: 10.1007/bf00271628. 6

R. Raguram and J.-M. Frahm. Recon: Scale-adaptive robust estimation via residual consensus. In *International Conference on Computer Vision (ICCV)*, 2011. DOI: 10.1109/iccv.2011.6126382. 56

R. Raguram, J.-M. Frahm, and M. Pollefeys. A comparative analysis of ransac techniques leading to adaptive real-time random sample consensus. In *European Conference on Computer Vision (ECCV)*, 2008. DOI: 10.1007/978-3-540-88688-4_37. 56

J. Rasmussen. Risk management in a dynamic society: A modelling problem. *Safety Science*, 27 (2): 183–213, 1997. DOI: 10.1016/s0925-7535(97)00052-0. 7

A. Rattani, W. J. Scheirer, and A. Ross. Open set fingerprint spoof detection across novel fabrication materials. *IEEE Transactions on Information Forensics and Security*, 10 (11): 2447–2460, 2015. DOI: 10.1109/tifs.2015.2464772. 88

J. H. Reynolds, T. Pasternak, and R. Desimone. Attention increases sensitivity of V4 neurons. *Neuron*, 26 (3): 703–714, 2000. DOI: 10.1016/s0896-6273(00)81206-4. 6

T. Riopka and T. E. Boult. Classification enhancement via biometric pattern perturbation. In *IAPR Audio- and Video-based Person Authentication (AVBPA)*, volume 3546, pages 850–859, 2005. DOI: 10.1007/11527923_89. 30, 32

E. Rosch, C. B. Mervis, W. D. Gray, D. M. Johnson, and P. Boyes-Braem. Basic objects in natural categories. *Cognitive Psychology*, 8: 382–439, 1976. DOI: 10.1016/0010-0285(76)90013-x. 5

Y. Rosseel. Mixture models of categorization. *Journal of Mathematical Psychology*, 46 (2): 178–210, 2002. DOI: 10.1006/jmps.2001.1379. 2

J. N. Rouder and R. Ratcliff. Comparing categorization models. *Journal of Experimental Psychology: General*, 133 (1): 63–82, 2004. DOI: 10.1037/0096-3445.133.1.63. 8

P. J. Rousseeuw and A. M. Leroy. *Robust Regression and Outlier Detection*, volume 589. John Wiley & Sons, 2005. DOI: 10.1002/0471725382. 7

E. M. Rudd, L. P. Jain, W. J. Scheirer, and T. E. Boult. The extreme value machine. *CoRR*, abs/1506.06112, 2015. http://arxiv.org/abs/1506.06112 95

O. Russakovsky, J. Deng, H. Su, J. Krause, S. Satheesh, S. Ma, Z. Huang, A. Karpathy, A. Khosla, M. Bernstein, A. C. Berg, and L. Fei-Fei. Imagenet large scale visual recognition challenge. *International Journal of Computer Vision*, 115 (3): 211–252, 2015. DOI: 10.1007/s11263-015-0816-y. 34, 71

T. Sattler, B. Leibe, and L. Kobbelt. SCRAMSAC: Improving RANSAC's efficiency with a spatial consistency filter. In *IEEE International Conference on Computer Vision (ICCV)*, 2009. DOI: 10.1109/iccv.2009.5459459. 56

W. J. Scheirer and T. E. Boult. A fusion-based approach to enhancing multi-modal biometric recognition system failure prediction and overall performance. In *IEEE International Conference on Biometrics: Theory, Applications, and Systems*, 2008. DOI: 10.1109/btas.2008.4699339. 30

W. J. Scheirer, A. Bendale, and T. E. Boult. Predicting biometric facial recognition failure with similarity surfaces and support vector machines. In *Proc. of the IEEE Workshop on Biometrics*, 2008. DOI: 10.1109/cvprw.2008.4563124. 30, 32

W. J. Scheirer, A. Rocha, R. Michaels, and T. E. Boult. Robust fusion: Extreme value theory for recognition score normalization. In *European Conference on Computer Vision (ECCV)*, September 2010. DOI: 10.1007/978-3-642-15558-1_35. 21, 26, 48, 49, 54, 55

W. J. Scheirer, A. Rocha, R. Michaels, and T. E. Boult. Meta-recognition: The theory and practice of recognition score analysis. *IEEE Transactions on Pattern Analysis and Machine Intelligence*, 33 (8): 1689–1695, August 2011. DOI: 10.1109/tpami.2011.54. 2, 8, 19, 21, 24, 26, 31, 32, 33, 36, 37, 40, 41, 58, 60

W. J. Scheirer, N. Kumar, P. N. Belhumeur, and T. E. Boult. Multi-attribute spaces: Calibration for attribute fusion and similarity search. In *IEEE Conference on Computer Vision and Pattern Recognition (CVPR)*, June 2012a. DOI: 10.1109/cvpr.2012.6248021. 2, 8, 21, 68, 69, 70

W. J. Scheirer, A. Rocha, J. Parris, and T. E. Boult. Learning for meta-recognition. *IEEE Transactions on Information Forensics and Security*, 7: 1214–1224, August 2012b. DOI: 10.1109/tifs.2012.2192430. 30, 41

W. J. Scheirer, A. Rocha, A. Sapkota, and T. E. Boult. Toward open set recognition. *IEEE Transactions on Pattern Analysis and Machine Intelligence*, 35 (7): 1757–1772, 2013. DOI: 10.1109/tpami.2012.256. 71, 81, 89, 90

W. J. Scheirer, L. P. Jain, and T. E. Boult. Probability models for open set recognition. *IEEE Transactions on Pattern Analysis and Machine Intelligence (T-PAMI)*, 36, November 2014a. DOI: 10.1109/tpami.2014.2321392. 2, 7, 8, 21, 70, 79, 88

W. J. Scheirer, M. Wilber, M. Eckmann, and T. E. Boult. Good recognition is non-metric. *Pattern Recognition*, 47: 2721–2731, August 2014b. DOI: 10.1016/j.patcog.2014.02.018. 34

B. Schölkopf, J. C. Platt, J. Shawe-Taylor, A. J. Smola, and R. C. Williamson. Estimating the support of a high-dimensional distribution. *Neural Computation*, 13 (7): 1443–1471, 2001. DOI: 10.1162/089976601750264965. 73

H. S. Scholte, S. Ghebreab, L. Waldorp, A. W. M. Smeulders, and V. A. F. Lamme. Brain responses strongly correlate with Weibull image statistics when processing natural images. *Journal of Vision*, 9 (4), 2009. DOI: 10.1167/9.4.29. 2, 6

G. Shakhnarovich, J. W. Fisher, and T. Darrell. Face recognition from long-term observations. In *European Conference on Computer Vision (ECCV)*, 2002. DOI: 10.1007/3-540-47977-5_56. 33

Z. Shi, F. Kiefer, J. Schneider, and V. Govindaraju. Modeling biometric systems using the general pareto distribution (GPD). In *SPIE Defense and Security Symposium*, pages 69440O–69440O. International Society for Optics and Photonics, 2008. DOI: 10.1117/12.778687. 19, 26

J. D. Smith and J. P. Minda. Distinguishing prototype-based and exemplar-based processes in dot-pattern category learning. *Journal of Experimental Psychology: Learning, Memory, and Cognition*, 28 (4): 800, 2002. DOI: 10.1037//0278-7393.28.4.800. 4

R. L. Smith. Extreme value theory based on the r largest annual events. *Journal of Hydrology*, 86 (1-2): 27–43, 1986. DOI: 10.1016/0022-1694(86)90004-1. 17

L. R. Squire and B. J. Knowlton. Learning about categories in the absence of memory. *Proc. of the National Academy of Sciences*, 92: 12470–12474, 1995. DOI: 10.1073/pnas.92.26.12470. 4

R. O. Stehling, M. A. Nascimento, and A. X. Falcão. A compact and efficient image retrieval approach based on border/interior pixel classification. In *International Conference on Information and Knowledge Management*. ACM, 2002. DOI: 10.1145/584810.584812. 55

J. A. Stirk and G. Underwood. Low-level visual saliency does not predict change detection in natural scenes. *Journal of Vision*, 7 (10): 1–10, July 2007. DOI: 10.1167/7.10.3. 5

A. Stuart, J. Ord, and S. Arnold. *Kendall's Advanced Theory of Statistics, Volume 2A: Classical Inference and the Linear Model*. Hodder Arnold, London, UK, 1999. 65

C. Szegedy, W. Zaremba, I. Sutskever, J. Bruna, D. Erhan, I. Goodfellow, and R. Fergus. Intriguing properties of neural networks. In *International Conference on Learning Representations*, April 2014. 9

E. Tabassi, C.L. Wilson, and C.I. Watson. Fingerprint image quality, NFIQ. In *National Institute of Standards and Technology, NISTIR 7151*, 2004. DOI: 10.6028/nist.ir.7151. 29

J. W. Tanaka and O. Corneille. Typicality effects in face and object perception: Further evidence for the attractor field model. *Perception and Psychophysics*, 69 (4): 619–627, May 2007. DOI: 10.3758/bf03193919. 5

J. W. Tanaka and M. J. Farah. Parts and wholes in face recognition. *Quarterly Journal of Experimental Psychology A: Human Experimental Psychology*, 46: 225–245, 1993. DOI: 10.1080/14640749308401045. 5

J. W. Tanaka and V. B. Simon. Caricature recognition in a neural network. *Visual Cognition*, 3 (4): 305–324, December 1996. DOI: 10.1080/135062896395616. 5

J. W. Tanaka, M. Giles, S. Kremen, and V. B. Simon. Mapping attractor fields in face space: The atypicality bias in face recognition. *Cognition*, 68: 199–220, October 1998. DOI: 10.1016/s0010-0277(98)00048-1. 5

J. W. Tanaka, T. L. Meixner, and J. Kantner. Exploring the perceptual spaces of faces, cars and birds in children and adults. *Dev. Sci.*, 14 (4): 762–768, July 2011. DOI: 10.1111/j.1467-7687.2010.01023.x. 5

J. W. Tanaka, J. Kantner, and M. S. Bartlett. How category structure influences the perception of object similarity: The atypicality bias. *Frontiers in Psychology*, 3: 1–11, June 2012. DOI: 10.3389/fpsyg.2012.00147. 2, 5

A. Tewari and P. L. Bartlett. On the consistency of multiclass classification methods. *Journal of Machine Learning Research*, 8 (May): 1007–1025, 2007. DOI: 10.1007/11503415_10. 67

B. Tordoff and D. W. Murray. Guided sampling and consensus for motion estimation. In *European Conference on Computer Vision (ECCV)*, 2002. DOI: 10.1007/3-540-47969-4_6. 59

P. H. S. Torr and A. Zisserman. MLESAC: A new robust estimator with application to estimating image geometry. *Computer Vision and Image Understanding*, 78 (1): 138–156, 2000. DOI: 10.1006/cviu.1999.0832. 56

C.-Y. Tsai and D. D. Cox. Are deep learning algorithms easily hackable? 2015. http://coxlab.github.io/ostrichinator/ 9

D. Tsao and M. Livingstone. Mechanisms of face perception. *Annual Review of Neuroscience*, 31: 411–437, July 2008. DOI: 10.1146/annurev.neuro.30.051606.094238. 2, 6

Z. Tu. Learning generative models via discriminative approaches. In *IEEE Conference on Computer Vision and Pattern Recognition (CVPR)*, 2007. DOI: 10.1109/cvpr.2007.383035. 6

A. Tversky.   Features of similarity.   *Psychological Review*, 84 (4): 327–352, 1977. DOI: 10.1037//0033-295x.84.4.327. 8

A. Tversky and I. Gati. Similarity, separability, and the triangle inequality. *Psychological Review*, 89 (2): 123–154, 1982. DOI: 10.1037//0033-295x.89.2.123. 8

A. Tversky and D. J. Koehler. Support theory: A nonextensional representation of subjective probability. *Psychological Review*, 101 (4): 547, 1994. DOI: 10.1037//0033-295x.101.4.547. 8

I. Ulusoy and C. M. Bishop. Generative versus discriminative methods for object recognition. In *IEEE Conference on Computer Vision and Pattern Recognition*, pages 258–265, 2005. DOI: 10.1109/cvpr.2005.167. 6

T. Valentine. A unified account of the effects of distinctiveness, inversion, and race in face recognition. *The Quarterly Journal of Experimental Psychology Section A: Human Experimental Psychology*, 43 (2): 161–204, May 1991. DOI: 10.1080/14640749108400966. 5

W. Vanpaemel and G. Storms. In search of abstraction: The varying abstraction model of categorization. *Psychonomic Bulletin and Review*, 15 (4): 732–749, 2008. DOI: 10.3758/pbr.15.4.732. 4

W. E. Vinje and J. L. Gallant. Sparse coding and decorrelation in primary visual cortex during natural vision. *Science*, 287 (5456): 1273–1276, 2000. DOI: 10.1126/science.287.5456.1273. 1

G. Wallis, U. E. Siebeck, K. Swann, V. Blanz, and H. H. Bülthoff. The prototype effect revisited: Evidence for an abstract feature model of face recognition. *Journal of Vision*, 8 (3): 1–15, 2008. DOI: 10.1167/8.3.20. 4

P. Wang, Q. Ji, and J. Wayman. Modeling and predicting face recognition system performance based on analysis of similarity scores. *IEEE Transactions on Pattern Analysis and Machine Intelligence*, 29 (4): 665–670, 2007. DOI: 10.1109/tpami.2007.1015. 30

Z. Wang, A. C. Bovik, Hamid R. Sheikh, and E. P. Simoncelli. Image quality assessment: From error visibility to structural similarity. *IEEE Transactions on Image Processing*, 13 (4): 600–612, 2004. DOI: 10.1109/tip.2003.819861. 29

A. B. Watson. Probability summation over time. *Vision Research*, 19 (5): 515–522, 1979. DOI: 10.1016/0042-6989(79)90136-6. 6

J. Wright, A. Y. Yang, A. Ganesh, S. S. Sastry, and Y. Ma. Robust face recognition via sparse representation. *IEEE Transactions on Pattern Analysis and Machine Intelligence*, 31 (2): 210–227, 2009. DOI: 10.1109/tpami.2008.79. 90

I. Yildirim, T. D. Kulkarni, W. A. Freiwald, and J. B. Tenenbaum. Efficient and robust analysis-by-synthesis in vision: A computational framework, behavioral tests, and modeling neuronal representations. In *Annual Conference of the Cognitive Science Society*, 2015. 96

H. Zhang and V. Patel. Sparse representation-based open set recognition. *IEEE Transactions on Pattern Analysis and Machine Intelligence*, 2017. DOI: 10.1109/tpami.2016.2613924. 89, 90

P. Zhang, J. Wang, A. Farhadi, M. Hebert, and D. Parikh. Predicting failures of vision systems. In *IEEE Conference on Computer Vision and Pattern Recognition (CVPR)*, 2014. DOI: 10.1109/cvpr.2014.456. 30

R. Zhang and D. Metaxas. Ro-svm: Support vector machine with reject option for image categorization. In *British Machine Vision Conference*, pages 1209–1218, 2006. DOI: 10.5244/c.20.123. 72

X. Zhou and T. S. Huang. Relevance feedback in image retrieval: A comprehensive review. *Multimedia Systems*, 8 (6): 536–544, 2003. DOI: 10.1007/s00530-002-0070-3. 73

S. C. Zhu. Statistical modeling and conceptualization of visual patterns. *IEEE Transactions on Pattern Analysis and Machine Intelligence*, 25 (6): 691–712, 2003. DOI: 10.1109/tpami.2003.1201820. 6

V. Zografos and R. Lenz. Spatio-chromatic image content descriptors and their analysis using extreme value theory. In A. Heyden and F. Kahl, Eds., *Image Analysis*, volume 6688 of *Lecture Notes in Computer Science*, pages 579–591. Springer Berlin Heidelberg, 2011. DOI: 10.1007/978-3-642-21227-7. 6

Author's Biography

WALTER J. SCHEIRER

Walter J. Scheirer is an Assistant Professor in the Department of Computer Science and Engineering at the University of Notre Dame. Previously, he was a postdoctoral fellow at Harvard University, with affiliations in the School of Engineering and Applied Sciences, Department of Molecular and Cellular Biology and Center for Brain Science, and the director of research & development at Securics, Inc., an early-stage company producing innovative computer vision-based solutions. He received his Ph.D. from the University of Colorado and his M.S. and B.A. degrees from Lehigh University. Dr. Scheirer has extensive experience in the areas of computer vision and human biometrics, with an emphasis on advanced learning techniques. His overarching research interest is the fundamental problem of recognition, including the representations and algorithms supporting solutions to it.

Printed in the United States
by Baker & Taylor Publisher Services